Sir Bobby Charlton

There have been some enormous figures in the history of Manchester United, but I think it's fair to say that none have been more influential or important than Sir Matt Busby.

When I first came to the club as a 15-year-old, I dealt with our assistant manager, Jimmy Murphy. It was Jimmy who taught me how to be a professional footballer in my formative years, but though I had little contact with Matt at that point, his aura was all around the club and everybody knew who the boss was.

I will always remember my first proper conversation with him, when I was an 18-year-old pushing to get into the first team. I was summoned to his office – which always meant you were in for either very good news or very bad news – and he asked me about an injury I was carrying.

I told him that it was absolutely fine and he responded by smiling and telling me that I would be making my debut against Charlton Athletic the following day. It wasn't fine, of course, but I got by, simply by avoiding the use of my injured foot where possible, and it seemed to work well enough because I scored twice and we won!

But the fear I felt while I was in Matt's office that day was the kind of feeling he evoked in people. Everyone was scared of him because he had this aura about him. Everyone knew he was in charge, and everyone respected that.

He was a fantastic manager, of course, and it was a joy to be part of his teams over such a long period of time. The idea of playing exciting, attacking football ran through the club, and it's just magic when I hear our supporters still singing his name to this day.

He didn't just manage the football team; he also managed the business side of the club. If you look around Old Trafford today at all the hospitality boxes, Matt introduced that to English football after witnessing it in San Francisco. It was only a few boxes at first, nothing like we have now, but Matt started the process because he recognised that Manchester United had to try to be the first to do everything.

That ethos and spirit has been a part of the club ever since, and all that Manchester United is, is a monument to a great man who wanted it to be the very best.

Sir Bobby Charlton

Contents

EDITORIAL TEAM **EDITOR-IN-CHIEF** Ian McLeish **FEATURES EDITOR** Steve Bartram
EDITORS Ben Ashby, Paul Davies **MANAGING EDITOR** Charlie Ghagan
Written by Ben Ashby, Steve Bartram, Steve Morgan, Giles Oakley, Ivan Ponting
PHOTOGRAPHY Getty, PA Photos, Mirrorpix

PUBLISHED BY Trinity Mirror Sport Media **MANAGING DIRECTOR** Steve Hanrahan
COMMERCIAL DIRECTOR Will Beedles **EXECUTIVE EDITOR** Paul Dove **EXECUTIVE ART EDITOR** Rick Cooke
SUB-EDITORS Adam Oldfield, Harri Aston, Gary Gilliland
DESIGNERS Chris Collins, Mark Frances, Adam Ward, Colin Sumpter
SENIOR MARKETING EXECUTIVE Claire Brown
PRINTED BY Buxton Press

Trinity Mirror Sport Media

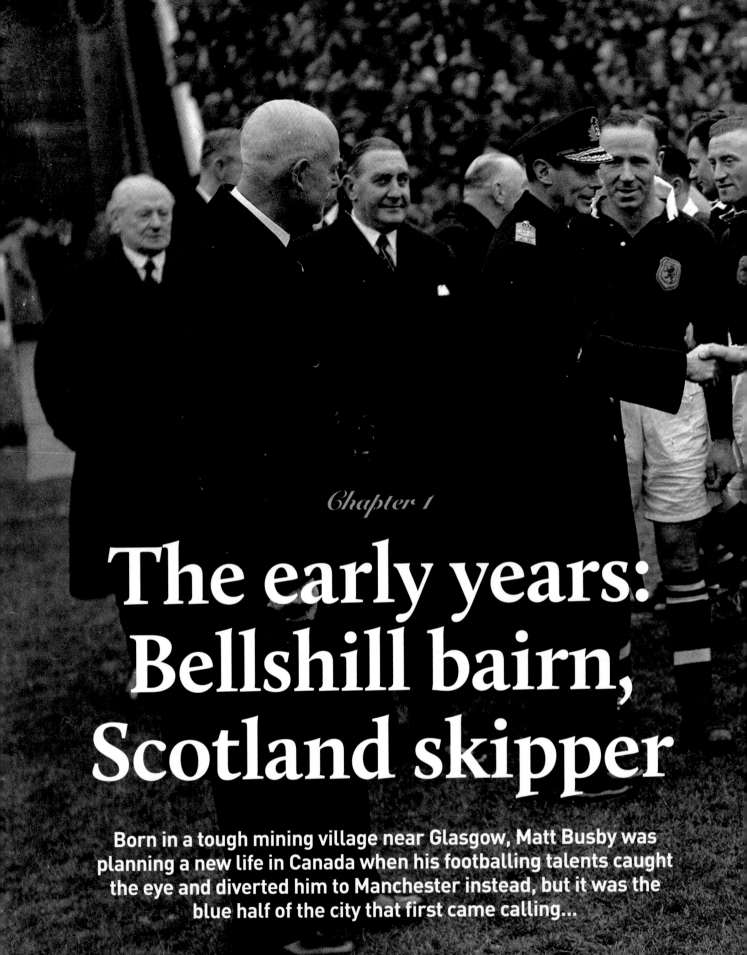

Chapter 1

The early years: Bellshill bairn, Scotland skipper

Born in a tough mining village near Glasgow, Matt Busby was planning a new life in Canada when his footballing talents caught the eye and diverted him to Manchester instead, but it was the blue half of the city that first came calling...

Matt Busby in his Manchester City playing days; (previous page) Scotland captain Busby introduces his team to King George VI before an England game at Wembley, 1944

"A footballer has come to this house this day." So proclaimed a doctor, stood in a small cottage in the mining village of Orbiston, Bellshill, south-east of Glasgow on 26 May 1909, exactly 90 years to the day before Manchester United scaled the highest of football's peaks with the dramatic capture of an unparalleled Treble triumph. Alexander Matthew Busby had arrived, and though the doctor's words would prove prophetic, he could have had no idea as to the impact this newborn would have on the world game – at Old Trafford especially.

The gritty reality of life in Orbiston was a million miles away from any vision of such glorious splendour. The first child of Nellie and Alex, Matt was followed by three sisters in ensuing years, and he soon became the sole male presence in his household, after his father was killed by a German sniper during the First World War.

The burden of responsibility subsequently heaped onto the youngster's shoulders would ultimately shape his character into that of a mature and empathetic leader. The old head resting on his shoulders was swiftly recognised by his school teachers, who noted that he could have a future on the other side of the teacher's desk and recommended that he enrol in a Motherwell grammar school at the age of 12.

Though Nellie concurred and duly switched her son's schooling, young Matt was to leave education after he turned 16, at which point he followed the village tradition of working in the pits in order to supplement his mother's income.

"There were only two ways for boys to go in those days: down, working in the pits, or up, if you happened to be good at football," he later reflected. Fortunately for Busby,

Pictured, top left, with
his City team-mates
in April 1934

he displayed enough natural ability in the
fiercely-contested games around his village
to warrant a call-up to Alpine Villa, the
area's eminent youth team. Success in the
under-18 Scottish Cup catapulted Busby
to the attentions of a wider audience, but
religious beliefs stood in the way of making
the grade in Scotland. His impressive work

"My application for a visa was delayed. Instead of emigrating to Canada, I emigrated to Manchester"

on trial at Rangers was undone when they
discovered that he was of Catholic faith,
while Celtic withdrew their interest upon
learning that he had trialled at Ibrox.

Busby's burgeoning career was growing
before a background of uncertainty, with
his family planning to emigrate. A move
to the United States or Canada was put on
hold pending a visa application, and the
ensuing months of lag opened the window
of opportunity in which Matt's future
became clear. "My application for a visa
was delayed at that time, and that delay

changed the whole course of my life," he
later admitted. "Instead of emigrating to
Canada, I emigrated to Manchester."

But rather than the Red of United, it was
the Blue of City in which Matt took his
first steps in English football. Moving down
to Manchester at 18, against his mother's
wishes, Busby struggled to acclimatise,
finding particular issues with both the pace
of the game and his deployment at inside-
half. Writing to his future wife, Jean, he
confessed: 'I feel that I am out of my sphere
in football', and he subsequently admitted
after his retirement: "I had decided that if
much was to be made of me, then it would
appear I would have to try some career
other than football."

Three years on and still struggling to
break into City's reserves, Busby was the
subject of interest from United. Chief scout
Louis Rocca, a man with a renowned eye
for a player, was scuppered by the Reds'
inability to stump up any kind of transfer
fee for the young Scot.

Fortune decreed that Matt would
get his opening at Maine Road after a
triallist didn't report in time to play at
right half-back for City's third team,
and Busby duly thrived in the position.

Manchester City's 1934
FA Cup-winners, with
Busby stood to the left
of keeper Frank Swift

Though occasionally found wanting in his defensive duties – a lack of pace proving his undoing – his brilliance going forward, and particularly his ability to disguise his impending use of the ball, soon marked him out as one of the position's leading exponents.

That prompted his installation as a first-team fixture at City, where he featured in their 1933 FA Cup final defeat to Everton and went on to gain his first Scotland cap, before going one better in the 1934 Cup final and starring in the Blues' 2-1 win over Portsmouth at Wembley.

That Cup final success proved to be the zenith of Busby's City career, and injuries, poor form and growing desire for a new challenge prompted him to leave for struggling Liverpool in March 1936. Newly-installed manager George Kay duly made his £8,000 signing captain and the pair helped inspire a late-season revival to avoid relegation.

The *Liverpool Echo* was swift to herald the newcomer. "Busby goes far up, if so inclined, and when he starts his upward trend, one knows his command of the ball will be such he will not be dispossessed," it reported in September 1936. "He is the richest and most practised passer the game has ever known. Hence he appears in a blinding light when compared with some other half-backs."

"He is the richest and most practised passer the game has ever known"

That upward trend in Liverpool's fortunes continued, and Busby thrived at Anfield in an all-Scottish half-back line alongside Tom Bradshaw and Jimmy McDougall for three seasons before, in August 1939, the onset of the Second World War led to his enlistment in the Army.

His absence from the game was short-

Clockwise from top right: Busby in his Army uniform with Joe Mercer of Everton, left, and Don Welsh of Charlton Athletic; shaking hands with England captain Stan Cullis in his role as Scotland skipper, and appearing for pre-War Liverpool

lived, however, following the War Office's ruling that footballers should continue to play, but simply represent the nearest club in the Wartime League rather than their parent club. Having initially been sent to Aldershot, where he became a non-commissioned officer, Company Sergeant-Major Instructor Busby went on to represent Reading, Chelsea, Aldershot and Hibernian during his various wartime postings. He also captained Scotland, briefly managed Hibs and was already scheduled to helm the British Army's team in a tour of Italy and the Middle East when news broke that the war was over.

Matt saw out the tour, but had plenty to consider as he prepared to be demobbed. Six months earlier, he had received a letter from United's Louis Rocca enquiring as to his plans. Penned on 15 December, 1944, the letter tantalised: "I don't know if you have considered about what you are going to do when war is over, but I have a great job for you if you are willing to take it on."

PLAYING CAREER

Manchester City (1929-1936)
Appearances: 227
Goals: 14
Honours: FA Cup (1934)

Liverpool (1936-1945)
Appearances: 122
Goals: 3
Honours: None

Total
Appearances: 349
Goals: 17

*excludes Wartime League

Chapter 2

Laying the foundations

Aged just 35, Matt Busby accepted an offer to become Manchester United manager, and he immediately set about turning a side of talented individuals into a winning team

"I had no doubt about my technical knowledge", Busby would later admit, long after his managerial career had ended. "Professional footballers are apt to be very confident about these things."

That assured attitude would come across when the Scot met with James W Gibson, United's owner, on 15 February 1945, to discuss the club's offer. During the course of negotiations, as Busby outlined the scale of the job he would be undertaking, the proposed three-year contract was amended to a five-year deal. United had their man, and Matt had the responsibility he craved. The nature of the meeting allowed for no doubt at all over who would be in charge of managing the club.

"Call it confidence, conceit, arrogance, or ignorance, but I was unequivocal about it," he said. "I would accept the managership of Manchester United only if they would let me have it all my own way. In those days the manager had the title and usually everybody else made the decisions. Directors chipped in with their ideas of picking a team, and niggled when, umpteen people having poked their noses and opinions in, a team emerged and inevitably differed from their several choices. As the manager I would want to manage. I would be the boss. This being so I would not have any excuse if I failed. Nor would I offer any. They could kick me out."

At the age of 35, the Scot had already crystallised the theory to which his managerial methods would adhere, inspired in part by the atmosphere he had experienced during his time with Liverpool; a family feel in stark contrast with the fractious unrest he had experienced behind the scenes at Manchester City.

"I had my theories about the psychology

Matt Busby with directors Walter Crickmer, James Gibson and George Whitaker; (above) bomb-damaged Old Trafford pictured shortly after the end of the Second World War; (previous page) Johnny Carey receives the FA Cup from King George VI at Wembley in 1948

needed for management, footballer-management; the essential qualities I felt had been missing in the game as I had known it," he said. "Perhaps my background had made me a little older than my years but, long before I became established, long before I was captain of Scotland, long before I moved from Manchester City to Liverpool, I vowed that if I ever became a manager I would respect players as individuals who needed individual treatment and thereby try to inspire respect from them."

Back at Anfield, meanwhile, Liverpool had been waiting on Busby's response to an invitation to work on the coaching staff under manager George Kay. When he opted to accept United's offer, there was confusion on Merseyside as he was still registered as a Liverpool player, but the situation was resolved in order to allow the Scot to start work as United manager when he was demobbed from the Army on 22 October 1945.

The Manchester United Busby joined was in a sorry state. Old Trafford had been bombed four years earlier and would not be repaired and fit for purpose until the start of the 1949/50 season, leaving the Reds to play their home games at Maine Road, the home of Manchester City. Furthermore, despite the generous financial backing of Gibson, the club was in a poor fiscal state.

And so, on his first day in office, Busby did not skip into Old Trafford and

Arsenal goalkeeper George Swindin prepares to repel a header from Jimmy Delaney during the Division One clash at Maine Road in 1948, watched by a record crowd of 83,260; (below) Jimmy Murphy, who became Busby's trusted aide; (far right) tracksuit manager Busby oversees training

perch himself behind a suitably grand desk. Rather, he took a pew around a mile away in one of the small offices of Cornbrook Cold Storage, one of Gibson's other businesses. Also within its confines were club secretary Walter Crickmer, his assistant Les Olive and a typist who had been borrowed from Cornbrook. Nevertheless, the confines could not coop Busby's ambition: "In that small office there was not much room for dreaming, or much time," he said. "But dream I did."

One aspect of the club which was to Busby's liking was the Manchester United Junior Athletic Club, or MUJAC, a youth system introduced by Gibson and Crickmer before the onset of the Second World War and designed at ensnaring the best young talents in the area. They, like Busby, recognised the benefits of nurturing talent, rather than purchasing it, and the United squad he inherited most certainly required an influx of fresh-faced verve.

Of the 11 players who started Busby's first game in charge the following August, the age range encompassed Jack Crompton (23) up to Jack Warner (33), with several players already in their mid-20s prime. That included captain Johnny Carey. The Irishman was the only squad member of whom Busby had any prior awareness, and the boss set about getting to know his charges as best he could. Several players were still spread about various locations on military service, and Busby could only train his squad on Tuesday and Thursday evenings. He emerged as the first tracksuit manager in football, donning sportswear to partake in training with his players. "That is where you get to know your fellows best – at work," he reasoned.

"At once I told them we would aim for the sky," he revealed, "because even then I decided that if you aim for the ceiling you might hit it and land straight on to your backside. I inherited a group of top-class talents, some of them great talents. I did

not inherit a team, as some would have it. If eleven talents automatically equalled one team, there would be no need for managers. In fact, great talents need more managing. They were not mere boys. The ones I had were probably as good as could be got together under one club boss anywhere – if we really did get together."

While Busby recognised the need to strengthen his playing ranks, he would not be rushed into spending the club's dwindling money reserves – even if benefactor Gibson was keen to bring in new blood. Rather, the first new recruit of the Busby reign was a 36-year-old, Service-grizzled Welshman. Jimmy Murphy had been a regular opponent during the Scot's playing career, a fiercely competitive presence in the West Bromwich Albion midfield who moved Busby to remark to a Liverpool team-mate: "You always need to wear two pairs of shinpads when you play against this chap." Nevertheless, a respectful friendship had grown between

the pair during their intertwined playing days and, six years after the War had halted football, they crossed paths again in Bari, Italy. Busby, who had already accepted the United job but was seeing out his role as manager of the Army football team,

once we seemed to fit," said Busby. Reds goalkeeper Harry Gregg later went one step further, speculating: "Jimmy Murphy and Matt Busby together could have climbed Everest. Matt made Jimmy and Jimmy made Matt. They needed each other."

"If you fancy a job when you are demobbed, Jimmy, come and look me up at Old Trafford"

watched from afar as Murphy, who ran an army sports centre during the conflict, addressed a group of players with his customary enthusiasm. Upon finishing his speech, Murphy noticed Busby marching towards him. "If you fancy a job when you are demobbed, Jimmy," said the Scot, "come and look me up at Old Trafford."

A year on, the Welshman arrived in Manchester to start work. "Almost at

Murphy was set to work managing the club's Reserves, and assisting in training with the first team. Bert Whalley was installed as his assistant. Soon, the playing squad included Jimmy Delaney, a Scottish international forward whose £4,000 transfer fee prompted murmurs among some who thought he was past his best. Instead, the 30-year-old brought pace, intellect and a flourish to an already

beguiling forward line. At the time, United's customary formation was a 2-3-5 approach. Bold, perhaps, but as Murphy put it: "It would have been ridiculous to have pulled seven or eight men back in defence with such a fine forward line as Delaney, (Johnny) Morris, (Jack) Rowley, (Stan) Pearson and (Charlie) Mitten at your disposal. With such an attack the only reasonable policy in those days was to use their great skills in trying to score goals."

A return of 95 goals in 42 First Division games during the 1946/47 season bore out that attacking mantra, but although the Busby era began with five straight wins – including a 5-0 win over Liverpool – it would be the Merseysiders who ended the campaign as champions. For United, the runners-up position would become a familiar berth over the following years. As

well as Busby's first season at the helm, his second, fourth and fifth campaigns ended with the Reds in second spot to Arsenal, Portsmouth and Tottenham respectively. The only exception was a fourth-place finish in 1949/50; not that the fare on show was cause for concern for those in charge.

"Manchester United in the immediate post-war years were a brilliantly entertaining side," reflected Murphy. "With Johnny Carey as the skipper, this mature team was our golden asset, for they gave us time and breathing space to look around and build for the future."

Short-term success for Busby's first United team arrived at the end of the Scot's second season in office, with victory over Blackpool in the 1948 FA Cup final; the club's first success in the competition since 1909. The road to Wembley began

Charlie Mitten battles with Blackpool right-back Eddie Shinwell during the opening stages of the 1948 FA Cup final; (below) a stub of a prized final ticket

Johnny Carey and the Cup are held aloft after a memorable 4-2 victory over Blackpool

with a typically frenetic 6-4 win over Aston Villa in the third round, and continued with the somewhat calmer overpowering of Liverpool (3-0), Charlton Athletic (2-0), Preston North End (4-2) and Derby County (3-1). In the final awaited Blackpool, then replete with the famed talents of Stanley Matthews, Stan Mortensen and company, and the two exciting, incisive sides set about treating Wembley to a showpiece

"Manchester United in the immediate post-war years were a brilliantly entertaining side"

spectacle which remains part of Cup final folklore to this day.

Busby's pre-match gameplan of keeping the ball on the United right – as far away from Matthews as possible – eventually bore fruit as Blackpool, who twice took the lead, were overcome in the latter stages,

and goals from Pearson, John Anderson and a Rowley brace secured a famous 4-2 win for the Reds. "A great team by any standards," was the manager's assessment of his trophy-winning heroes.

United's youngest starter at Wembley, Morris, would soon bring out the sterner side of his manager, however. When the gifted youngster disagreed with his exclusion from the team in 1949, he was soon on his way to Derby County for £25,000 – a then-world record fee for the first sale of the Busby era. Morris learned the hard way that conflict was not something the boss shied away from – something those behind the scenes had learned in his early months in the role. Watching a game from the directors' box during his first season in charge, Matt heard his team selection being loudly queried by a club director. When he duly came face-to-face with the director in question in the toilets, he stressed: "Never dare to say anything like that to me when other people can hear you." None – even

Stan Pearson, left, alongside Jack Rowley; (right) Johnny Carey leads his team on to the pitch – and to the 1952 title

owner Gibson – were left in any doubt as to who was in charge, and within long it was accepted throughout the club that Busby had the final say on all things team related. As Harold Hardman, Gibson's successor as chairman, put it in a board meeting: "Our manager has asked us for advice and we will give it to him, and then he'll please his bloody self."

Busby's way was backed to the hilt and it was finally validated by the league title in 1951/52, the Reds' 50th campaign in the Football League. Though punctuated heavily by two World Wars, a 41-year wait for domestic rule was becoming a millstone for a team so increasingly accustomed to finishing just behind the champions. In the end, it was nothing new or innovative which ended the Reds' barren run, with the success built upon the goals of strikers Rowley and Pearson, and the leadership of skipper Carey. A 16-game unbeaten league run between mid-November and late March teed up the success, and as the campaign wore on, only Arsenal and Tottenham could keep pace.

By the final day of the season, the Gunners arrived at Old Trafford for a title showdown which, in reality, was a foregone conclusion in advance of kick-off. The visitors required a 7-0 win to snatch the title on goal difference but, although they did partake in a game of seven goals, they could only muster one of them as Busby's men strode to glory.

> "Our manager has asked us for advice and we will give it to him, and then he'll please his bloody self"

Injury reduced Arsenal to just 10 men early on, by which point Rowley had already opened the scoring. Stan Pearson and Roger Byrne struck before the interval, while 'Gunner' completed his hat-trick after the break and teed up Pearson for a last-minute tap-in. Within long, supporters flooded onto the field to celebrate with the champions, much to the chagrin of the

Champions again
after 41 years
– Johnny Carey
leaves the pitch
following United's 6-1
thrashing of Arsenal
to confirm the 1952
title; (below) Johnny
Berry, who joined
from Birmingham as
Busby rebuilt
an ageing side

Beswick Prize Band, whose attempts to strike up *See the Conquering Hero Comes* were scuppered.

"Red-faced bandsmen could be seen struggling for their lives to get out of the crowd, holding aloft tubas and trombones, cornets and euphoniums, lest these too should be crushed flat in the press," observed Donny Davies, of the *Manchester Guardian*.

Slightly more refined revelry would take place later in the day, as Busby took his players to Manchester Town Hall for a civic reception in which skipper Carey took to the piano to entertain the merrymakers. But while the skipper was calling the

tune on the night, the ringing of changes was growing in volume. The team was unquestionably ageing. Carey and Pearson were 33, Chilton 34, Rowley had become the first player in the club's history to reach 30 goals in a season, but had surpassed that figure in age a year earlier, a year before Henry Cockburn. The Reds' top five appearance makers in their title season were all in their fourth decade.

Busby had taken steps to bring down the age of his side by promoting Byrne from the youth team, while Johnny Berry had joined from Birmingham for a club record fee of £25,000, but while the sprightly pair pepped up the Reds' approach, the manager

was well aware that his champions would require substantial revamping in order to enjoy longer-term success.

"The future for a manager is fraught with danger, especially a manager of a championship team," warned the boss. "If he wins the First Division Championship, he cannot go any higher and the odds are that he will go lower. And, given five years or so, he will go straight down and out, he on his backside, the club into a division or two below. Unless he has made other arrangements. Like thinking ahead... at least five years ahead."

Which stems back to a conversation Busby had enjoyed with Murphy at the end of their first season at the club, the 1946/47 campaign. An end-of-season function had been arranged to celebrate the first team's second-placed finish and the Reserves' successful tilt at the Central League championship. Noticing that his right-hand man was far from his usual jovial self, Busby enquired as to why. The Welshman confessed to a sense of failure that there were no players in his squad of sufficient quality to improve the Reds' senior side. Having considered Murphy's answer, Busby paused before retorting: "In that case, we will have to find and develop our own youngsters."

THE ROAD TO BUSBY'S FIRST TROPHY

United's path to FA Cup glory in 1948 was lined with six ties against top-flight opposition, but Busby's Reds powered through each obstacle in a frenzied, 22-goal campaign to end a four-decade barren spell in style...

Third round
Aston Villa 4 (Edwards 1, 46, Smith 70, Dorsett pen 81)
United 6 (Rowley 15, Morris 17, 32, Pearson 30, 88, Delaney 42)

Fourth round
United 3 (Rowley 30, Morris 35, Mitten 37)
Liverpool 0

Fifth round
United 2 (Warner 25, Mitten 85)
Charlton Athletic 0

Quarter-final
United 4 (Mitten 23, Pearson 33, 78, Rowley 80)
Preston North End 1 (McIntosh 44)

Semi-final
Derby County 1 (Steel 42)
United 3 (Pearson 30, 34, 55)

Final
Blackpool 2 (Shimwell pen 14), Mortensen 35)
United 4 (Rowley 30, 70, Pearson 75, Anderson 85)

Busby's Leaders

While Busby was always the boss, he also had his deputies. We profile the 10 men who he made United captain during his reign

JOHNNY CAREY
Captain: 1945-1953

The highly respected 'Gentleman' John arrived at Old Trafford aged 17 in 1936 from St James' Gate in Dublin. By the time Sir Matt took the reins he was 26 years old with two league seasons and a ton of wartime football under his belt. Busby chose the dependable Irishman as his first skipper, and was rewarded with seven seasons of stalwart captaincy. Carey led the Reds to 1948 FA Cup glory and the 1952 league title. His versatility meant he filled virtually every position for United at some point – including a match in goal.

United appearances/goals: 344/17

STAN PEARSON
Captain: 1953-1954

Pearson's United career closely mirrored that of Carey, earning his stripes in the two seasons prior to the Second World War before becoming one of Busby's stalwarts when league football resumed. When Carey retired at the close of the 1952/53 campaign, Busby looked to his experienced forward to don the mantle of captain for the next season, even though Pearson was to be less of a consistent fixture on the pitch during the campaign than he had been in the preceding years.

Appearances/goals: 343/148

ALLENBY CHILTON
Captain 1954-55

With the ageing Pearson having moved on to Bury, it was the turn of another of Busby's post-war lynchpins to pick up the captaincy baton. Having outstayed Pearson, who had outstayed Carey, it was now Chilton's honour to captain the side for one season, his last at the club. All three of Busby's first skippers were born within five months of one another and had similarly stellar careers under him as pillars in what was his first great side.

Appearances/goals: 391/3

ROGER BYRNE
Captain: 1955-58

When Chilton left towards the end of the 1954/55 season to become Grimsby Town's player-manager, again Busby turned to his defence for his next leader, but this time chose someone younger. Roger Byrne had not long turned 26, in his fourth season in the first team, when Busby appointed him skipper. During his tenure, Byrne was the respected senior figure of Busby's new generation of exciting young players, the Babes, and led the precocious side to consecutive titles in 1956 and 1957.

Appearances/goals: 280/20

BILL FOULKES
Captain: 1958-59

After the Munich tragedy had robbed United of a generation of players that included skipper Byrne, Bill Foulkes took on the United captaincy in the difficult times that followed. The rock-solid defender proceeded to lead his makeshift team to a Wembley FA Cup final and European Cup semi-final in May 1958, sterling achievements in the circumstances, even in defeat.

Appearances/goals: 688/9

DENNIS VIOLLET
Captain: 1959-60

Foulkes was succeeded in the captaincy by Dennis Viollet, the prolific inside-forward who had been a fixture in the team since the 1952/53 campaign. It was in his single term as captain that Viollet set the club record mark of 32 goals scored in a single league season, which still stands today.

Appearances/goals: 293/179

MAURICE SETTERS
Captain: 1960-63

The next man Busby appointed as his leader on the field was Setters, the tough, no-nonsense half-back, signed from West Brom in 1960. He took the captaincy in his first full season with the Reds, and his was a vocal and vigorous style of leadership, driving his team-mates on with barked commands and encouragement.

Appearances/goals: 194/14

NOEL CANTWELL
Captain: 1963-67

Cantwell was already an experienced pro when Busby signed him from West Ham in late 1960, aged 28. As a full-back, respected figure and natural leader of men, he fitted the profile of several of his manager's previous skippers, and was duly made club captain in 1963, going on to lift the FA Cup in May that year. Though Cantwell was to become an infrequent fixture in Busby's side, he kept his club captain role – while Denis Law took over in his stead on the pitch – because of his leadership qualities.

Appearances/goals: 146/8

DENIS LAW
Captain: 1964-68

The 'King' became the next in Busby's prestigious lines of captains, sharing duties with Cantwell and becoming the figurehead out on the pitch. The ace scorer and European footballer of the Year had the proud honour of lifting league titles in both 1965 and 1967 as Busby's third great team came to fruition, with Denis at the heart of it alongside Bobby Charlton and George Best.

Appearances/goals: 404/237

BOBBY CHARLTON
Captain: 1968-73

Busby could not have chosen his final captain better. Charlton had been alongside his manager at Munich and it was completely fitting that it should be he who captained the side to the emotional 1968 European Cup triumph at Wembley 10 years on. Bobby's seniority, experience and influence on the pitch gave him iron-clad captaincy credentials and he remained skipper after Busby's retirement as manager.

Appearances/goals: 758/249

Chapter 3

The birth of the Babes

An enriched vision of success swelled Busby's thoughts as United ended the 41-year wait for domestic dominance. In the next evolutionary phase, the pioneering Scot nurtured a new batch of young, home-grown hotshots who would go on to emulate their title-winning forebears

Bert Whalley, left, and Jimmy Murphy, right, helped shape Busby's second great side; (previous page) the manager, at home on the training ground

"My old team had won the championship. It looked a bit chancy to chop it to bits," reflected Matt Busby, of the transition from his first great United side to the second. But hack away he did, ending up with the team that would be the hallmark of his career in football.

While the Scot and assistant Jimmy Murphy had been masterminding the Reds' 1951/52 title triumph, the club's conveyor belt of home-grown talent had been cranked into overdrive, thanks largely to the sterling work of a trio of backroom staff affectionately known as 'The Three Musketeers': Murphy, coach Bert Whalley and Joe Armstrong, who had become chief scout following predecessor Louis Rocca's death in 1950. Overseen by Busby, the threesome continued the vision of James Gibson and Walter Crickmer, who had established the Manchester United Junior Athletic Club 15 years earlier. John Aston and Stan Pearson had been the youth system's first success stories, taking their place in the 1948 FA Cup-winning side,

and by the time they both departed the club either side of the 1953/54 campaign, they left behind a United side awash with contemporaries who had followed their footsteps up through the ranks.

"With Matt superintending operations, we three lieutenants set off on what was destined to be one of the most thrilling episodes of my life," reflected Murphy. "Matt reasoned, why pay such exorbitant fees if it were possible to spot footballers still in their early teens and bring them to Manchester United where they could be groomed in our style? Great Britain is a gold mine of the finest all-round footballers in the world, so why not dig into this gold mine?"

For Busby, the chance to save

"Matt reasoned, why pay such exorbitant fees if it were possible to spot footballers still in their early teens and bring them to Manchester United?"

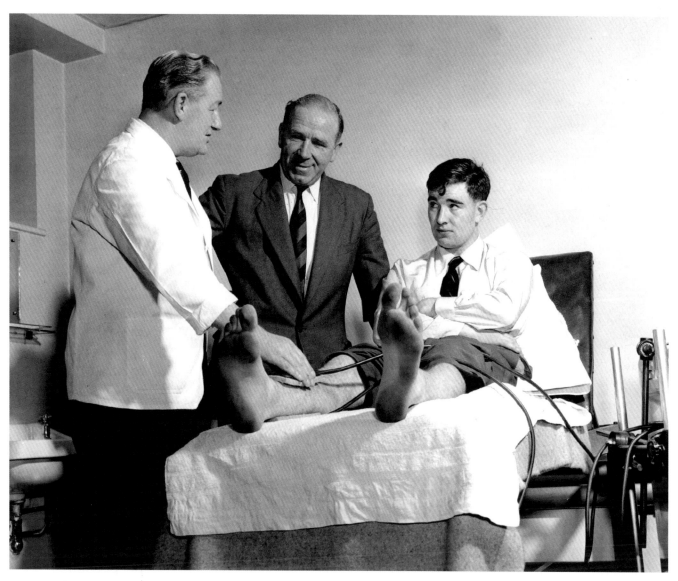

Whalley tends to Jackie Blanchflower, who was brought through the United youth system; (below) the Reds take on Chelsea as the 1952/53 season swings into action, a campaign in which there would be nine debuts signalling a changing of the guard

money was secondary to a long-held professional ambition. "From the start of my managership, and even before, I had envisaged my very own nursery or crèche," he later revealed. "The pre-war method of team-building was to wait for weakness to occur and try to repair it by buying a player or finding an outstanding one from junior football. Teenagers were a sensation if they made a First Division team.

"In 1946 it was revolutionary even to think about getting boys straight from school. Get them early enough, I thought, and they would be trained according to some sort of pattern; in my case, the pattern I was trying constantly to create at Manchester United, in the first team and any other team, so that if a boy came through as far as his ability, courage, speed and character were concerned, he would fit into the pattern without feeling like a stranger among people painting pretty pictures he did not understand and had never seen before."

Scouts and informants – or 'soccer spies', as Murphy termed them – were stationed around Great Britain and detailed with keeping United aware of any twinkling talents whose star might have the chance to shine at Old Trafford. Youngsters brought to the United bosom were encouraged to embrace the club in return, being made aware of their surroundings and their part within a collective. "Matt's ideal was to create at Old Trafford the sort of spirit one gets in a school team in which players grow up together, and

Busby puts his problem-solving skills to good use as he helps Blanchflower with a crossword puzzle; (below) more fledgling members of the first-team squad unwind, among them Liam Whelan, Mark Jones, Gordon Clayton, Alan Rhodes and Duncan Edwards

know one another both on and off the field," explained Murphy. "A fanatical schoolboyish pride in the club – this was the ultimate aim. It was not enough to have a group of fine young footballers; they had to have a sense of belonging."

Perhaps as a natural part of that process, Busby adopted a role that went beyond the customary player-manager relationship when dealing with the club's younger players. Jackie Blanchflower, who had debuted midway through the 1951/52 title triumph, had been met by the Scot at Manchester's Victoria train station as soon as he had arrived from Belfast. The young Ulsterman – then just 16 – was taken to his new manager's house and fed before being taken on a tour of Old Trafford. "He was like a father, a very kind, quiet man who looked after us like we were his own," the centre-half recalled.

Busby had his own theory as to his patriarchal inclinations. "Whether the loss of my father had subconsciously given me a feeling of being unprotected, I do not know," he said. "Certainly there is some gap for a boy without a father when all other boys around him could talk about theirs incessantly, and did. Perhaps it induced in me some paternal, protective feeling for other unfortunate or sensitive young people.

"It would have been ungrateful – no, immoral – for me to talk parents into allowing their boys to come along to Manchester to live and to play football if I had not immediately assumed responsibility for their well-being. So I became their foster father, a huge responsibility and one that was never far from my mind. I had to care how they were going on. They had to see I cared for how they were going on. I do not know any greater joy in football than to see first the seed show through, then the lissom shoot growing, then the healthy young plant and finally the full bloom and hear the acclaim that attends it. Then and only then can the football foster-father join in with the parents and say: 'That's my boy.'"

Roger Byrne was one of the foremost figures to graduate to the senior ranks during the early '50s. Here he is at White Hart Lane in November 1952, a year on from his first-team breakthrough

An overlapping aspect of both his managerial and paternal capacities was Busby's interest in his youngsters' extracurricular activities. Though the Scot stopped short of having spies dotted around the Manchester area, he made it clear to his young players that word of any wrongdoing or unacceptable behaviour would inevitably filter back to him.

"Matt seemed to know everything that went on," admitted Wilf McGuinness. "He had us in many times saying: 'I know where you were last night. The problem is, you might only have a couple of drinks, a lager and lime, but by the time it gets back

stalemate: "I feel Manchester United have some of the best prospects in the country and Roger and Jackie took their chances well. They have been kicking at the first-team door for some time."

Byrne, who had the ability to easily turn his hand to a variety of sports and had opted not to pursue a promising junior career in cricket, admitted: "There were indeed times when I regretted the move into professional football. It was only when injuries cropped up that I managed to get into the Reserves. However, encouraged by Matt Busby, I was patient and just as he promised, my chance came."

"The marks of the nursery cradle were still on them, but they did not show"

to me it's five or six pints, so watch what you're doing.'"

When they behaved, however, the rewards would be forthcoming. Blanchflower and Roger Byrne were both sufficiently trusted to make their senior bows in the hotbed atmosphere of a goalless draw at Anfield in November 1951. Their efforts prompted *Manchester Evening News* scribe Frank Nicklin to use the 'Busby Babes' sobriquet for the first time, and though Busby felt it maligned their maturity – he poetically observed: "The marks of the nursery cradle were still on them, but they did not show" – he was moved to admit after the Merseyside

If Byrne's tale taught the benefits of patience, it also came to demonstrate the manner in which youngsters would be accommodated in the senior side once they were deemed ready. Initially deployed as a full-back for his debut and the ensuing 18 games, the Gorton-born talent was moved to outside-left for the final six games of the title run-in and duly notched seven goals. In time, having expressed his misgivings at being stationed so far forward, he would migrate back to become one of his generation's leading full-backs, but Byrne's rotation merely confirmed the management team's open-mindedness over the use of their players in their formative

Coming man Byrne heads clear against Millwall in the FA Cup in January 1953, while stalwart Johnny Carey looks on; (below) Tommy Taylor was a key arrival at Old Trafford, adding goals galore

stages. "Over the years we have always gone in for this policy of switching positions until a boy found his rightful place," Murphy later reflected.

Such patience was not as prevalent up on the terraces, however. At first-team level, the 1952/53 term began in such sluggish fashion in terms of results that supporters began to vocally criticise Busby and his staff, whose champions were next to bottom midway through October and had suffered three successive defeats. "Those of us at the heart of affairs could see a glimmer of light," said Murphy, while the manager calmly reassured shareholders that there was no need to panic, with talent in the ranks worth at least £200,000, in his estimation. The Scot's fiscal sense was borne out over the ensuing years; United didn't spend a single penny in the transfer market between March 1953 and December 1957, a run ended by the arrival of goalkeeper Harry Gregg from Doncaster.

The signing in 1953 was a key chapter in the story of the Babes, as the Reds' fledgling talents were supplemented by the high-profile recruitment of Tommy Taylor, a bashful goal machine with Barnsley who had been the subject of interest from 20 other clubs in the Football League. While Murphy felt that Busby's charm swayed the 21-year-old Yorkshireman United's way, the manager felt differently as to why Taylor and many of the other youngsters were so keen to come to Old Trafford.

"I believe they wanted to come to Manchester United because we had won a reputation for being the best club for the best boy players," he said. "Not all were set on joining United before all others. Then Joe Armstrong, Jimmy Murphy or

Busby's Babes start to take flight as Johnny Berry, Duncan Edwards, Mark Jones, Roger Byrne and Dennis Viollet reach for the sky in training; (above left) Taylor nets for the Reds against Chelsea at OT; (far right) 16-year-old Edwards leaves the pitch following his United debut against Cardiff

I would try talking them into believing how good we were as a club for the best boys. We didn't sign all the best ones, but we managed more than our share, so that in our midst, ever maturing, ever growing into the Old Trafford pattern of play and behaviour, we had an extraordinary number of youths."

While Taylor notched twice on his debut – ending the 1952/53 campaign with seven goals in 11 games and going on to register the best goals-per-game average of any in the pantheon of great United strikers – the crown jewel among the club's young talents was widely acknowledged to be Duncan Edwards. For all the sterling work of United's scouting network, it was a tip-off from Joe Mercer, then coaching the England schoolboy team, that alerted Busby to the talents of the youngster rated the pride of the Midlands. Though coveted by Wolverhampton Wanderers, themselves already building great repute as a hotbed

for top young talents, Edwards had been overheard by Mercer saying that he wanted to play for United. Busby received word and promptly made his move. Upon introducing himself, the Scot met the response: "I think Manchester United is the greatest team in the world. I'd give anything to play for you."

The manager's sales patter was not required, and Edwards went on to make his

> ## "Apart from Matt's plain statement that United had players worth £200,000, we kept quiet and waited, just like a gardener has to wait for little apples to grow"

Reds bow in April 1953, aged 16, and though a 1-4 home defeat to Cardiff City was hardly an ideal baptism for the powerful prodigy, Matt was unmoved. A week later, a local

young striker named Dennis Viollet was the next debutant in a 2-1 win at Newcastle. "I stuck it out," said Busby. "The future was more important than the present that season." By the end of term, Edwards and Viollet were among nine players – alongside Taylor, Jack Scott, Eddie Lewis, David Pegg, John Doherty, Bill Foulkes and Les Olive – to have taken their bow during the campaign. Not that Busby and company were shouting loudly about the evolution their squad was undergoing.

As Murphy recalled: "Apart from Matt's plain statement that United had players worth £200,000, we kept quiet and waited, just like a gardener has to wait for little apples to grow. Managing a football club is a little like gardening; you cannot rush nature any more than you can rush young footballers before they are ripe for the demanding challenge of first-class soccer.

"One by one these boys were given a run in the first team to see how they shaped.

United's 1955 FA Youth Cup-winning team, including Duncan Edwards, Shay Brennan, Eddie Colman, Wilf McGuinness and Bobby Charlton; (left) Charlton performs his household chores, aged 15, in the days before becoming a household name

It didn't happen overnight, because Matt, like the shrewd general he is, would not risk ruining a boy's confidence or his career by plunging him too quickly into First Division soccer, the toughest competition in the world. Visualise seven years of hard work and planning, years of unremitting endeavours by men such as Bert Whalley, Joe Armstrong and all our scouts. At the end of it, there on the field, were the youngsters who in three short seasons were to put Manchester United on top again."

An almost inevitable by-product of the

"We had to peer through the mist, but what I saw was enough for me. This boy is going to be a world-beater"

steady stream of fledgling talents entering United's books was success at youth level. The FA Youth Cup had undergone its maiden campaign in 1952/53, and was won in emphatic fashion as United trounced Wolves 9-3 over two legs. Of the 11 players who represented the Reds across that tie, three had already made their first-team debuts and another seven would go on to emulate them. Managed by Murphy,

United won five successive Youth Cups, going unbeaten in the competition between its 1952 inception and the Munich disaster. Murphy used 33 players in those five finals, 21 of whom appeared for Busby's first team.

One of them, perhaps the most famous of all the Babes, arrived on the Reds' radar on 9 February 1953. Joe Armstrong, upon returning from a scouting trip to the north-east, reported back to Old Trafford with what Murphy termed "the excitement of a gold prospector who has struck it rich". Though the wintry conditions had not aided his reconnaissance work, Armstrong confided: "We had to peer through the mist, but what I saw was enough for me. This boy is going to be a world-beater."

Armstong's intuition was spot-on. The boy – Robert Charlton – went on to hold Manchester United's appearances and goals records in tandem for 35 years, winning three First Division titles, one European Cup and one FA Cup with United, the World Cup with England and the Ballon d'Or. The Reds had stolen a march on countless other suitors when Armstrong approached Charlton immediately after the game that February day to state his club's interest, and Joe continued to develop United's advantage over the following months.

Roger Byrne leads out the Reds after taking over captaincy duties from Allenby Chilton; (right) Ray Wood and Duncan Edwards thwart a Wolves attack at a snowy Molineux, as Busby's Division One leaders beat their third-placed rivals 2-0 to move closer to the league title

"In all the comings and goings of rival scouts, he was a regular presence around our house," recalled Charlton, "arguing persuasively that Manchester United had the greatest of futures and that it was at Old Trafford I would be best developed. They had so many fine young players come through and this was where the club had invested most seriously.

new young talent when he felt the timing was right. It was a huge story when he dropped half of his team and picked youngsters. Many predicted humiliation for United, but the new blood flowed strongly. When I read about the Old Trafford revolution in the newspaper I felt a great surge of excitement."

Charlton duly signed up for a role in the

"When I read about the Old Trafford revolution in the newspaper I felt a great surge of excitement"

"It was also true that in me, Joe had something of a captive audience. I lost something of my heart to his club in 1948 when they beat Blackpool in one of the classic FA Cup finals. I followed the course of that team with great interest, watched them reach a peak and then noted how Busby was indeed unafraid of introducing

revolution and watched on from the youth ranks as Busby's increasingly fresh-faced first team took a sizeable step forward, finishing fourth in the 1953/54 campaign. Skipper Johnny Carey had retired before the season and his replacement, Stan Pearson, departed Old Trafford at the end of it. Next in line was Allenby Chilton, but

the 37-year-old brought to an end his epic association with the club by hanging up his boots midway through the 1954/55 term.

Busby again sought to appoint from within, but plumped for a younger man to wear the armband, appointing the 26-year-old Byrne to the role. "Roger was the ideal choice as Busby's link between himself and the team," concurred legendary defender Bill Foulkes, himself a Babe who debuted in December 1952. "He did not possess the physical strength or presence of Allenby Chilton, but he was quick to help any of his team-mates, and as time went on he was also quick to voice his opinions to Matt if the occasion arose. Exchanges could become quite heated between the two, but they did have the perfect working relationship and had great respect for each other."

Chilton's departure also created a vacancy in the centre of defence, into which stepped granite-hewn Yorkshire lad Mark Jones, a keen amateur boxer who had considered a professional career in the ring. Jones had made just nine appearances since his debut as a 17-year-old in October 1950, but was an ever-present in the 13 games between Chilton's retirement and the end of the 1954/55 campaign. On the final day of the season, Jones was one of eight home-grown players in Busby's line-up, the remainder being signings Taylor, Ray Wood and Johnny Berry.

Fifth place was the reward for an entertaining but inconsistent season's work, but still those behind the scenes were unperturbed by finishing just five points behind champions Chelsea. "While Manchester United slipped slightly in the league in 1954 and 1955, waiting in the wings ready to leap into league football were the most brilliant batch of youngsters ever to be on one club's books at the same time," Murphy later smiled.

Just as Chilton had been the last link between the 1948 Cup-winners and the new-look United, only Byrne, Berry, Jones and Wood bridged the gap between the 1951/52 title-winners and the squad at

Tommy Taylor's winning goal against Blackpool had confirmed title success for United's 1955/56 squad; (below) Eddie Colman impressed the United management with his fluidity and flair

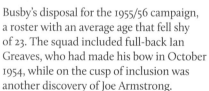

Busby's disposal for the 1955/56 campaign, a roster with an average age that fell shy of 23. The squad included full-back Ian Greaves, who had made his bow in October 1954, while on the cusp of inclusion was another discovery of Joe Armstrong.

"Put a grass skirt on him and you've got a hula-hula dancer," was Armstrong's summary of young Eddie Colman, the evasive winger who would earn the nickname 'Snakehips'. In Murphy's estimation, Colman was worthy of greater acclaim, labelling the Salford-born swayer "a genius". The Welshman continued: "Eddie was an original. No matter how I search my memory, I cannot recall another player with his particular flair or personality or that cheeky waggle of the hips as he swept past opponents. The years cannot dim my memories of him."

By the time Colman was tested at senior level, starting in November 1955's defeat at Bolton Wanderers, United were tied on points at the top of the First Division table with Sunderland and Blackpool. That Burnden Park reverse was the Reds' fourth of the league season, but Busby's boys would suffer just three more all term, sustaining a shock FA Cup exit at second-tier Bristol Rovers but winning 17 of the remaining 25 First Division games.

"Eddie was an original. No matter how I search my memory, I cannot recall another player with his flair or personality or that cheeky waggle of the hips"

From Babes to champions: captain Byrne holds aloft the Championship trophy

Stan Cullis' handy Wolves side were beaten home and away, defending champions Chelsea were pummelled 4-2 at Stamford Bridge and the Reds amassed a home record that yielded 18 wins and three draws from 21 games. Accordingly, United romped to the title by a staggering 11-point margin, a 20th-century record in the days when a win was worth just two points.

The club's fourth First Division success was confirmed on 7 April 1956 by a 2-1 victory over Blackpool, though Busby was forced to miss the coronation in order to attend the funeral of his mother-in-law – a bind he described at the time as his toughest decision during his time in football. Nevertheless, the Scot heralded: "A collection of kids the quality of which had never before, I believe, been assembled in one club anywhere in the world."

International recognition had beckoned several squad members, with England caps at various levels for seven Reds, plus Northern Ireland and Republic of Ireland caps for Blanchflower and inside-forward Liam Whelan respectively. The football world was widening for United's players, and that applied at club level, too. Wolves had partaken in high-profile friendly games against European club opponents over previous years, and United's title triumph had run parallel to the inaugural season of the European Cup. Champions Chelsea had been invited to represent English football, but had abstained under pressure from the country's football authorities. For a trailblazer like Busby, no such resistance would stop him and his gifted young stars from testing themselves against the best opponents the continent had to offer.

PROVIDING
A PLATFORM

A staggering 76 players made the step up from United's youth system to first-team duties under the management of Sir Matt Busby. Here's the full roll call, in order...

JOHN ROACH • JOE WALTON • CHARLIE MITTEN • JOHN ASTON SR • JOHNNY MORRIS • CLIFF COLLINSON • KEN PEGG • JOHN ANDERSON • SAMMY LYNN • LAURIE CASSIDY • BRIAN BIRCH • FRANK CLEMPSON • JEFF WHITEFOOT • THOMAS McNULTY • DON GIBSON • BILLY REDMAN • MARK JONES • CLIFF BIRKETT • JACKIE BLANCHFLOWER • ROGER BYRNE • JACK SCOTT • EDDIE LEWIS • DAVID PEGG • JOHN DOHERTY • BILL FOULKES • DUNCAN EDWARDS • DENNIS VIOLLET • LES OLIVE • NOEL McFARLANE • PATRICK KENNEDY • ALBERT SCANLON • FRED GOODWIN • GEOFF BENT • LIAM WHELAN • WALTER WHITEHURST • WILF McGUINNESS • EDDIE COLMAN • RONNIE COPE • BOBBY CHARLTON • TONY HAWKSWORTH • GORDON CLAYTON • ALEX DAWSON • DAVID GASKELL • KENNY MORGANS • MARK PEARSON • SHAY BRENNAN • BOBBY HARROP • JOE CAROLAN • REG HUNTER • JOHNNY GILES • NOBBY LAWTON • FRANK HAYDOCK • JIMMY NICHOLSON • NOBBY STILES • IAN MOIR • HAROLD BRATT • RONNIE BRIGGS • SAMMY McMILLAN • PHIL CHISNALL • DENNIS WALKER • GEORGE BEST • WILLIE ANDERSON • WILF TRANTER • ALBERT KINSEY • JOHN FITZPATRICK • JOHN ASTON JR • BOBBY NOBLE • JIMMY RYAN • BRIAN KIDD • FRANCIS BURNS • FRANK KOPEL • ALAN GOWLING • JIMMY RIMMER • CARLO SARTORI • STEVE JAMES • TOMMY O'NEIL

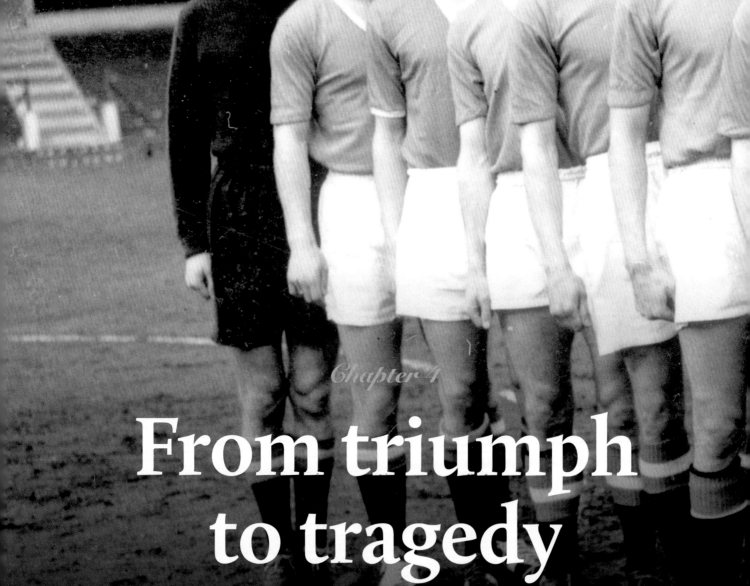

Chapter 4

From triumph to tragedy

Domestic title success opened the tantalising door to the continent – through which the pioneering Busby led his team into the European Cup, where immediate promise was followed by terrible misfortune

Visionaries regularly attract criticism from those who prefer to do things by the book. They laughed at Galileo; they sneered at Isaac Newton. If it seems a stretch to place Matt Busby in the orbit of such pioneering thinkers, the comparison is no quantum leap, especially amid the insular English football landscape of the 1950s. Despite the national team's mauling by a Hungary side that bewitched and bewildered in winning 6-3 at Wembley in 1953, inflicting a first international defeat on home soil, the view from the flat-earthers at the Football League remained intransigent. "Johnny Foreigner" had little to teach the inventors of *our* game, who had already boycotted three World Cups. It wasn't the future, it was merely a blip. Order would surely be restored.

To a man of adventure like Busby, such thinking was arrogant, unfathomable and unconscionable: like Galileo, he was looking at the stars. The boss had keenly watched the advent of the European Cup, contested for the first time in 1955/56, and was seduced by the exotica of mixing it with the Continental cream in midweek, floodlit matches – what greater challenge could there be? Chelsea, the English champions of 1955, had accepted the offer to enter the competition, but having been advised to "reconsider" by the FA, who discussed the matter for all of 15 minutes, they acquiesced.

A year on and this wouldn't do for Busby's league winners. His thrusting young lads – average age some 22 – had, in winning the title by a remarkable 11 points in 1956, already given the lie to much of the game's received wisdom, a wisdom predicated on a pre-war view favouring old pros that now seemed wholly arcane.

Clockwise from left: Matt Busby with Roger Byrne and Duncan Edwards; Dennis Viollet scoring his fourth goal against Anderlecht in the famous 10-0 win in the European Cup preliminary round, second leg, at Maine Road in September 1956; the manager at the airport before leaving for Cologne to watch the European Cup semi-finals draw in 1957

Football, and the world at large, was changing fast, and he wanted a ringside seat. Genial godfather he may have been, but he had an iron will when the mood took. "Prestige alone demanded that the Continental challenge should be met, not avoided," was his argument.

With the blessing of his chairman Harold Hardman and Football Association chief Stanley Rous, Busby held firm. United – with the caveat that it would not disrupt their league programme, a bargain that ultimately exacted a chilling price – accepted the offer of a place in the 1956/57 European Cup and set off on a path that would lead to glory; albeit a delayed glory, and one tinged with infinite poignancy.

Thus, United's European history began on 12 September 1956 with a 2-0 win in Belgium against Anderlecht. As Old Trafford was still without floodlights, the home leg was played at Maine Road. Landlords Manchester City predicted that only 10,000 would show, but the crowd was nearer 45,000; so much for the gimmickry of this new-fangled competition.

Mark Jones, left, and Bill Foulkes, right, defend
a cross against Athletic Bilbao in the home leg of
the 1956/57 European Cup quarter-finals

What that first home crowd saw had them hooked. United tore into their opponents, as if born for this moment. By half-time it was 5-0 and there was no let-up. It finished 10-0: still the biggest win in club history. Dennis Viollet hit four, strike partner Tommy Taylor three, Liam Whelan

excelled themselves that night. It was in fact the finest exhibition of teamwork I had ever seen from any side, either at club or international level," he purred.

These weren't just the words of a man keen to vindicate his own decision – they were shared by an opposition who had no

"We've played against the best teams of Hungary and Russia and never been beaten like this"

two and Johnny Berry got the other. Such was the bond between Busby's players that, when the score hit double figures, attention focused on trying to engineer a goal for David Pegg, who'd laid on five goals while darting from wing to wing.

For Busby, it was manna from heaven. "I was becoming accustomed to seeing the great team of those days play well, but they

answers, only admiration. Jef Mermans, Anderlecht's experienced Belgian international, was struck by United's refusal to stop attacking. "After United had scored their sixth, they still ran as hard as they had at the start," he said. "We've played against the best teams of Hungary and Russia and never been beaten like this."

Borussia Dortmund were dispensed

Keeper Ray Wood saves under pressure from Real Madrid's Alfredo di Stefano during the European Cup semi-final, first leg, at the Bernabéu in 1957; (right) the United programme for the visit of Athletic Bilbao

with next, by a narrower 3-2 aggregate, a five-goal affair at Maine Road following a stalemate in Germany. The Maine Road crowd this time was a massive 76,598. The quarter-finals brought a trip to northern Spain and Athletic Bilbao. Schooled, to an extent, by their Basque opponents – who hit three first-half goals in a 5-3 defeat – there was at least hope after Liam Whelan's late goal reduced the deficit. Advancing now would be tough, but after the showing against Anderlecht, not impossible. On a night that swiftly entered club folklore, United, roared on by another huge crowd, secured a memorable 3-0 success which had fans and journalists alike salivating. The game – in which Johnny Berry's 84th-minute goal secured United's progress – was beamed to picture houses across the city on a night so joyous and raucous it was later likened to VE Day. Once more, the boss was enthralled. "I have never known anything like this in my life," he said.

United's path to the 1957 final was blocked by Real Madrid, winners of the inaugural trophy. Once more the first-leg deficit was two goals, this time 3-1. In Old Trafford's first taste of floodlit action, the Reds were held 2-2 by the great Alfredo di Stefano and company. Though Busby was forced to accept second best for now, he still accentuated the positive. "A great experienced side will always triumph over a great inexperienced side," he mused.

It was hard to dispute: European football was here to stay, with United in the vanguard. Busby's pioneering poster boys would soon be crowned champions for a second season in a row, by eight points this time in 1956/57 (narrowly missing out on a historic league and FA Cup Double after a Wembley defeat to Aston Villa). They would be back in Europe to try their luck again in 1957/58, stronger for the experience. What could stand in their way?

The team prepare to board at Ringway Airport, Manchester, for the journey to Belgrade in 1958. Tragically, many would not make it home

Even players not directly involved in the early European action couldn't get enough. A 19-year-old Bobby Charlton – just a week before taking his first-team bow – hot-footed it from National Service in Shrewsbury to catch the thrashing of Anderlecht. Driven by his company sergeant-major in exchange for a free ticket, he recalled the powerful spectacle. "There were times when we looked at each other, shook our heads and murmured: 'unbelievable'. It was a wet and dreary night and the Maine Road floodlights had feeble candlepower, but my club-mates created a glow of their own.

"The effect of the [Bilbao] result swept beyond the boundaries of the city. Manchester and so much of the rest of English football had burst into new life. You could only guess at the reaction of Alan Hardaker, the man who had tried so hard to slam the door on Europe – and at the same time wonder why he had been so dead set against pushing back the boundaries of English football."

United entered the 1957/58 tournament confident it could be won. Shamrock Rovers of the Irish League were seen off by a commanding 9-2 aggregate in the preliminary round (6-0 at home, 3-2 away) and Dukla Prague were outclassed 3-0 at Old Trafford in the first leg, securing a safe passage to a post-Christmas quarter-final meeting with Red Star Belgrade. Busby's settled outfit was further strengthened by the arrival of Harry Gregg, then the world's most expensive goalkeeper, and there were plenty of others from the production line waiting in the wings – Charlton, for one, was now getting more regular first-team football. United's first-leg victory at Old Trafford was by a slender 2-1 margin. The second leg would be a tricky affair against opponents who would give no quarter on home soil, yet United travelled to Belgrade buoyant after registering a thrilling 5-4 First Division victory against Arsenal at Highbury (see panel, right).

A dream start against Red Star brought a goal from Viollet inside two minutes. Charlton then scored twice to put United into a seemingly impregnable position, 3-0 up, 5-1 on aggregate. After the break,

Harry Gregg makes a save watched by Duncan Edwards (arms outstretched) against Arsenal at Highbury – the last game before the fateful journey in February 1958

The last team photo, against Red Star Belgrade in the second leg of the European Cup quarter-final, before the air crash. From left to right: Duncan Edwards, Eddie Colman, Mark Jones, Ken Morgans, Bobby Charlton, Dennis Viollet, Tommy Taylor, Bill Foulkes, Harry Gregg, Albert Scanlon and Roger Byrne

A FINAL FLOURISH

Arsenal 4
Manchester United 5

Football League Division One
1 February 1958, Highbury

The Babes' final match on English soil entered the annals as a fitting sign-off from a side built to entertain with youthful abandon; a breathless game adorned with thrills, spills and a staggering nine goals.

Of the eight players claimed by Munich disaster just five days later, five started at Highbury and turned in a thrilling performance that showcased all that was charming about Busby's swaggering young side.

Just 10 minutes had passed when Duncan Edwards fired in a long-range effort, and Bobby Charlton followed suit before Tommy Taylor turned in from close-range to put the Reds three goals clear by the interval.

Perhaps displaying their naivety, the Babes were pegged back to 3-3 shortly after the hour as the Gunners struck three goals in an incredible four-minute spell. Yet, somehow, United dusted themselves down and quickly re-took the lead through Dennis Viollet, before Taylor hammered home a fifth with little more than 20 minutes remaining.

Though Arsenal rallied again to halve the arrears and make the scoreline 5-4, Busby's side learned from their mistakes and closed out the victory, before leaving the field to resounding applause from supporters desperate to salute both teams, but unaware that the victors would never again play together on English soil.

ARSENAL
Kelsey; Charlton, Fotheringham, Evans; Groves, Ward, Bowen, Nutt; Tapscott, Herd, Bloomfield
Goals: Herd 58, Bloomfield 60, 61, Tapscott 76

MANCHESTER UNITED
Gregg; Foulkes, Jones, Byrne; Morgans, Colman, Edwards, Scanlon; Charlton, Taylor, Viollet
Goals: Edwards 10, Charlton 34, Taylor 44, 71, Viollet 65

though, the hosts pegged one back, then another. Finally, just before the hour mark, they equalised: 3-3 now, just a goal behind. Despite the frayed nerves, United held on – a second successive semi-final was theirs. It had been some night; a stern examination of the young men's resolve in front of a volatile crowd on a snow-crusted surface. To celebrate, the team repaired for a well-deserved night out, first playing poker, before heading on to the home of a British embassy official. "It was all part of the great adventure that stretched before us so dazzlingly," Charlton recalled. "The toast, as it always was then, was to the future."

On the journey back, United's flight stopped to refuel at Munich airport. Ice and slush on the runway produced two abortive take-off attempts; the players passed the time with coffee dispensed by courier Bela Miklos' wife Eleanor, throwing snowballs, continuing their card games. The weather looked set against a third try – Duncan Edwards sent a telegram to his landlady

"It was all part of the great adventure that stretched before us so dazzlingly. The toast, as it always was then, was to the future"

warning her he might well be held over.

However, Busby was mindful of the need to return – part of the Football League's proviso for allowing United's entry to the European Cup was the insistence they be back at least 24 hours before their next fixture: in this case a crunch clash with table-topping Wolves, three points in the clear. Almost exactly a year before, United's players had scraped ice from the wings of the flight home from Bilbao. Busby, anxious to do the right thing, agreed they would give it one more try. Captain James Thain gave the signal to get back on board.

As the *Lord Burghley*, a British European Airways charter flight, struggled to get

Clockwise from left: a
seriously ill Matt Busby
receives treatment;
Harry Gregg and
Bill Foulkes visit
team-mate Ken
Morgans in hospital;
the crash site

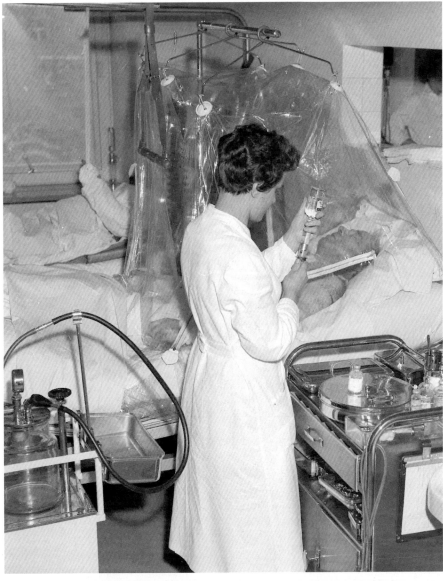

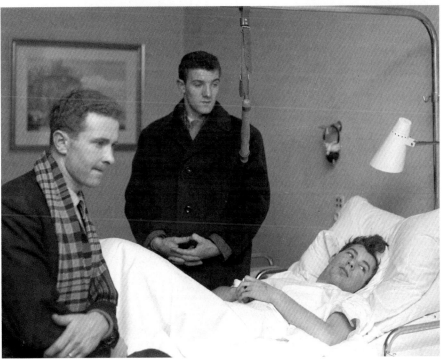

Clockwise from left: a
seriously ill Matt Busby
receives treatment;
Harry Gregg and
Bill Foulkes visit
team-mate Ken
Morgans in hospital;
the crash site

airborne, it rent the air with the straining
engines, careering off the slush-strewn
runway, skidding through the perimeter
fence and across the road. The fuselage was
ripped in two. Seven of the Babes, football's
shining stars – skipper Roger Byrne, at 28
the oldest in the side, fellow full-back Geoff
Bent (25), half-backs Eddie Colman (21)
and Mark Jones (24), and forwards Tommy
Taylor (26), Liam Whelan and David Pegg
(both 22) died outright, along with 14 more
of the 44 on board, including trainer Tom
Curry, coach Bert Whalley, secretary Walter
Crickmer, and eight local and national
journalists, including Frank Swift, a former
team-mate of Matt Busby at Manchester
City. Duncan Edwards and Busby were
critically ill, but clinging to life.

Back in Manchester – this, of course,
in the pre-digital age – the news broke
agonisingly slowly. Piece by piece, the
terrible details filtered through; an awful
jigsaw of facts gradually assembling an
unthinkable picture. Across the city, grief
descended like a heavy blanket. Factory
workers recalled the noise of machinery
grinding to an eerie halt. Youngsters who
had aped their heroes' weekend antics at
Highbury in school playgrounds struggled
to take it in. This couldn't be happening.
The team with the world at their feet,
who'd brought so much joy and pride, not
only to Manchester, but the nation at large,
snuffed out before their prime.

Edwards and Busby's struggle for life
became daily household topics – updates
anxiously awaited in the hope both would
somehow pull through. Twice Busby
received the Last Rites and, as he lay in
Munich's Rechts der Isar hospital, could
only contemplate how his dream – a vision
to taking Manchester United to the peak
of the continental game – had been cruelly
torn to shreds.

Chapter 5

United will go on...

The darkest day in the club's history had claimed the lives of many and set Busby's United back years, but the dignity and desire shown in the aftermath of this tragedy provided a fitting salute to those that had perished

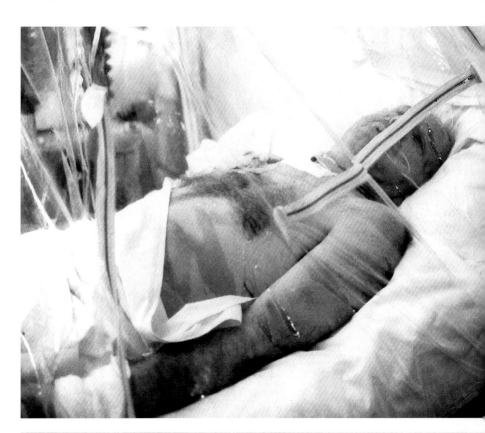

Manchester United's Phoenix-like rise from the ashes of Munich has sometimes been perceived as inevitable, as if ordained by destiny. But that is to underestimate all those who made sure United survived, and thrived. Their determination was rooted in the values embodied in Matt Busby and his legendary Babes.

The whole of Manchester was reeling with shock from news of the disaster which left Matt hovering between life and death. His assistant Jimmy Murphy, returning from international duty as manager of Wales, took over. Numbed with grief, he and relatives, including Busby's wife Jean, hastened to the Rechts der Isar hospital in Munich where Professor Georg Maurer's superb medical teams were tending to the survivors. Matt was in an oxygen tent with appalling injuries and his chances of survival were said to be '50:50'. His collapsed lung necessitated surgery without anaesthetic, yet somehow he managed to whisper to Jimmy, 'Keep the flag flying for me'.

Murphy saw all the injured players, including 21-year-old Duncan Edwards, universally admired as one of England's greatest players and much loved for his sweet, boyish nature. Duncan asked when kick-off was against title rivals, Wolves. When Jimmy replied: 'Three o'clock', Edwards simply urged: 'Get stuck in...'

The tough little winger Johnny Berry was in a coma, Jackie Blanchflower was severely injured and Bobby Charlton, Albert Scanlon, Ken Morgans, Dennis Viollet and Ray Wood were all receiving treatment. The only players fit to go home were goalkeeper Harry Gregg, hero of the plane crash, and defender Bill Foulkes. It was all too much for Murphy. Seven players had died and others suffered shockingly bad injuries, and Gregg came across the Welshman sobbing inconsolably. When the dead bodies were flown home it prompted extraordinary expressions of grief, with thousands lining the streets in silent homage. The outpourings of sorrow went far beyond Manchester and every day sacks of mail arrived from all over the world expressing sympathy.

(Previous page) Bill Foulkes leads out the Reds against Sheffield Wednesday in the first game after Munich; (right) Bobby Charlton recovers at the Rechts der Isar hospital; (left) Busby clings onto life; (below) a guard of honour as the victims of the air disaster are returned to British soil

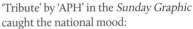

'Tribute' by 'APH' in the *Sunday Graphic* caught the national mood:

> *'Alas, the last long whistle blows,*
> *And still are all the twinkling toes,*
> *The leaping heads, the graceful arts,*
> *That thrilled the stands and fired the hearts.*
> *Win, lose or draw, their name was high;*
> *And "Busby's Babes" will never die.'*

The pall of sadness hanging over Manchester was so overwhelming, Murphy took the decision to move the players to Blackpool. Busby was kept oblivious of events as Professor Maurer insisted that the stricken manager couldn't withstand the shock of being told the whole story. Meanwhile, Captain Rayment, the co-pilot, died from his injuries.

As the life-and-death struggles continued, Reds chairman Harold Hardman confirmed that United would fulfil all scheduled fixtures. First came a postponed FA Cup fifth-round tie against Sheffield Wednesday, despite 17 players missing as a consequence of the crash. When Jimmy assembled his team to face Wednesday, 13 days after the crash, it was so last-minute the match programme had 11 blank spaces for the players' names. Led by the visibly traumatised Gregg and new

skipper Foulkes, the rest were Reserves and youth-teamers plus two newcomers, the FA having waived regulations to allow emergency signings. Inspired by Hardman's call to arms in the *United Review* – headlined 'United Will Go On' – almost 60,000 people jammed into Old Trafford, creating an intensely emotional, at times uncanny atmosphere. A lone voice repeatedly called out: 'Dun-can, Dun-can!'

The players in Munich listened to

squares commemorating the departed. The *Manchester Evening News* said the 'real hero' of this famous victory was Busby, for assembling such a wealth of reserve talent.

Any fleeting euphoria attained in victory was soon dashed when, two days later, Edwards lost his valiant struggle for life. A priest inadvertently let slip what had happened to Duncan, so Busby insisted on hearing the whole story. Jean sadly shook her head as he named players in turn.

"Dun-can, Dun-can!"

live relays of the game in the hospital dispensary. They heard 17-year-old debutant Shay Brennan score twice, with teenager Alex Dawson also netting in an astonishing 3-0 victory. Murphy was in tears along with countless others, including a girl with a scarf embroidered with the names of United players, black

Dangerously weak, Matt now entered the dark night of the soul, wanting nothing more to do with football.

Back home, however, United continued to go on. For the next Cup match, the Reds were strengthened by the return of Bobby Charlton. After holding West Bromwich Albion to a 2-2 draw the replay was one

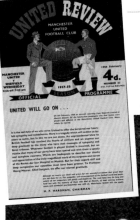

Harry Gregg makes a spectacular save to deny Fulham in the FA Cup semi-final at Villa Park; (below right) United fans prepare to cheer the Reds to victory in the semi-final replay at Highbury; (below) Alex Dawson in Cup action against West Brom; (left) the matchday programme for the first post-Munich fixture against Sheffield Wednesday

Jimmy Murphy greets Stan Crowther, signed less than an hour before the Reds took on Sheffield Wednesday and, top left, Shay Brennan's corner opens the scoring against the Owls

of the most enthralling matches ever witnessed at Old Trafford. The Baggies were no pushovers against a team which seemed to have the whole country behind them, and it was epic, end-to-end stuff, settled only in the dying seconds when Colin Webster scored from a glorious Charlton pass. Murphy called Busby to relay the news. All he could say was: "Wonderful, wonderful."

Days later the same teams met in the league at Old Trafford. Professor Maurer and his team were guests of honour, greeted with tremendous gratitude by the huge crowd. A tape recording of Matt's painfully weak voice was played before kick-off, thanking the German doctors for 'the wonderful treatment and attention' they had received. Many supporters wept, again, and the visitors won 4-0.

United faced Second Division Fulham in the Cup semi-final at Villa Park on 22 March. It was another thrilling encounter, in which Charlton hit two

thunderous goals in a 2-2 draw. United won the replay 5-3 four days later at Highbury, with Dawson scoring a hat-trick. There were hints that some of the younger players were running on empty, displaying mainly weary relief at the end that United had reached the Wembley final. The inspirational leadership of Murphy had made this possible, a glorious contribution to United's history.

By now Busby was off the danger list and Blanchflower and Berry were slowly recovering, although it became increasingly clear neither would play football again. Matt went home on April 18 – 71 days after the crash – after Jean, with almost perfect timing, quietly suggested to him that maybe he should return to football, because it was what the boys would have wanted. Miraculously, it did the trick. Perhaps he needed 'permission', being gripped by guilt over what had happened, a feeling he never lost. After all, he'd taken United into Europe, and he'd insisted on certain players

Busby thanks Professor Georg Maurer and his staff as he is discharged from hospital; (right) receiving a helping hand as he heads to the Wembley dressing rooms; (below) Harry Gregg saves from Nat Lofthouse, but the striker later scores twice to give Bolton the FA Cup

travelling, even though not selected to play.

"I just looked at the empty field," said Matt of his return to Old Trafford, "and I tell you I have never felt such a terrible vacuum. And so I cried." He attempted to address staff but broke down. There had been much suffering in his life before, but he had always kept that side hidden, though consistently displaying fatherly compassion and empathy towards others. After Munich his eyes betrayed unspoken grief, a look he never really lost.

Busby went to the Wembley Cup final, although he insisted Murphy should lead the team out. Bolton Wanderers won 2-0 with goals scored by Nat Lofthouse and were the better team, overcoming the romantic desire of millions to see United win. Graciously, painfully, Matt went into the Bolton dressing room to congratulate the winners.

When he resumed as manager for the next season, 1958/59, Busby cautioned that it would take United five years to

compete seriously for trophies again. It was thus a shock when things began well. Despite having lost 10 players through death and injury, United finished as runners-up to Wolves. There were some outstanding displays, such as the 6-1 defeat of Blackburn, one paper calling it 'a magnificent performance by United, who had no real weakness'. Matt signed the 'Golden Boy' Albert Quixall, for a record £45,000 and United became a thrilling attacking side, scoring 103 goals in the league, inspired by Busby's enduring charisma and the romance of United's unique story.

The following season, however, was less encouraging, the Reds finishing in seventh place. United again scored more than a hundred goals, but the defending was woeful, with 80 conceded, hence the recruitment of Maurice Setters, a rough-house half-back from West Bromwich Albion. Encouragingly there was wider exposure through TV highlights

(Right) Albert Quixall was one of Busby's first signings as he returned to his manager role for the 1958/59 season, while Bobby Charlton and Dennis Viollet provided some memorable moments in the seasons that followed

"I just looked at the empty field, and I tell you I have never felt such a terrible vacuum. And so I cried"

coverage on the BBC's *Sports Special*, forerunner of *Match of the Day*, which helped 'nationalise' United's appeal. Black and white pictures of a 5-1 away victory against Nottingham Forest were offset by a dreadful 7-3 home defeat by Newcastle United. There was always something compelling about United, even in defeat. A new crop of youngsters was introduced as United continued to attract large crowds. There were magical moments, such as

when Viollet scored twice in a 5-0 win at Fulham in March 1960, overtaking Jack Rowley's club record for league goals in a season. His eventual total of 32 goals has still never been bettered.

Season 1960/61 was just as frustrating, ending in the same dreary seventh place, even if one bright spot was the debut of future World and European Cup winner Nobby Stiles, featured in *Sports Special* coverage of a 1-1 draw with Bolton. Matt

repeatedly emphasised that United had been working to a five-year plan but discontent was mounting and attendances were dropping. In October 1960 the *Manchester Evening Chronicle* gave the Scot a platform to respond to his critics:

"We lost the services of 10 great players in that awful Munich disaster, and I only signed two replacements. In a way I consider it unfortunate that we had so much artificial success immediately after the crash. Had we slumped to the Second Division, people would have nodded their heads in sympathy, as such a fall was to be expected. But instead we continued with success that on the cards looked impossible to get. I succeeded in getting Albert Quixall and Maurice Setters. But eight other replacements were short, simply because

the players of Manchester United standard I wanted were not available. Eight players is a terrible lot. I am convinced that things will start clicking again and United will surprise many people who have been lying in wait for the days we would fail."

In a bid to inject further quality into the Reds' ranks, cultured full-back Noel Cantwell was signed from West Ham, but the frustration continued. United were maddeningly inconsistent; beating Double-winners Tottenham in January 1961, then losing 0-6 at Leicester just a week later and slipping to a shocking 2-7 FA Cup defeat at home to Sheffield Wednesday a further 10 days on. Meanwhile, Matt's emotional torment continued: "Deep down the sorrow is there all the time," he admitted. "You never really rid yourself of it. It

Alex Dawson and Dennis Viollet challenge Fulham goalkeeper Tony Macedo during the 1959/60 season

Nobby Stiles took his Reds bow during the 1960/61 campaign; (below) Noel Cantwell added quality at full back as Matt Busby continued team rebuilding

"Deep down the sorrow is there all the time. You never really rid yourself of it. It becomes part of you"

becomes part of you. You might be alone, and it all comes back to you, like a kind of roundabout, and you weep."

Success seemed even more elusive in season 1961/62, as United slumped to 15th place, the club's worst finish since the Second World War. David Herd, a high-scoring centre forward, was signed from Arsenal but his contribution was initially fitful and supporters were becoming ever more restive. When United went 10 successive matches without victory between late September and early December, Matt even received hate mail and 'poison pen letters'. He displayed a Zen-like grace, replying kindly to one schoolboy's supportive letter:

"Many thanks for your very nice letter which was indeed a tonic to me. Needless to say, I take no notice of cranks, but it is still nice to know we have some genuine supporters about. Good luck and God bless."

The season petered out, with United still no closer to success, despite an encouraging FA Cup run to the semi-finals. Matt remained remarkably calm, ignoring his physical pain and emotional exhaustion. The tortured years of failure had revealed another side of his greatness: his unbreakable spirit and courage. No-one ever talked of Munich at Old Trafford, but he would still sometimes see his 'boys' out on the pitch. But while the ghosts of the past would never truly disappear, the Scot would begin to see figures of the future out there as well.

When United fell to a lacklustre 0-2 defeat at Fulham in the final game of the 1961/62 campaign, few supporters were dispirited. Excitement had already pervaded the air, with the nation's newspapers awash with rumours that the Reds were about to sign an exciting young Scot by the name of Denis Law. The darkest night was gradually making way for the dawn.

Chapter 6

From Wembley '63 to Wembley '68

Five years on from Munich, Busby had rebuilt a Manchester United team capable of winning silverware again – and one that would go on to scale the ultimate European height that had become the holy grail of both manager and club

From previous page: Busby leads his United side out at Wembley to face Leicester City in May 1963

Matt Busby was still suffering, both physically and mentally, as he embarked on the 1962/63 campaign, a season that was to be a definitive watershed in the fortunes of the modern Manchester United. It heralded the birth of his third great team.

The wounds to his body that he had sustained at Munich had substantially healed but still gave him pain, of which he made light in public. Meanwhile he could never banish from his mind his despair over the 23 deaths that resulted from the disaster.

Even though the Old Trafford boss could not, by any reasonable reckoning, be blamed for the tragedy, he felt an unavoidable sense of responsibility because he was the man in charge – and the one who had so staunchly championed blazing the English trail into European football.

On his worst days, the 53-year-old Scot was afflicted by a debilitating bone-weariness when he contemplated the colossal task of building a new top-quality side. But such was his passionate commitment to the club, and to the memory of the young men who had lost their lives, quitting was never a viable option.

After four years of steady work since the accident – helping to maximise the talents of promising youngsters such as full-backs Shay Brennan and Tony Dunne, utility man Nobby Stiles and inside-forward-cum-winger Johnny Giles, while enjoying acceptable if not sensational success in the transfer market – Busby made a mammoth step towards his ultimate goal in the summer of 1962 with the signing of Denis Law.

Still only 22, the pencil-slim Aberdonian with a puckish dash of devilry which verged

Clockwise from above: Busby with his record bargain Denis Law; Denis rounding goalkeeper Gordon Banks – although he didn't convert the chance – in the 1963 FA Cup final against Leicester; Law's fellow strike signing David Herd punishing his former club, Arsenal

on villainy at times, was already among the most brilliant strikers on the planet. And he wasn't enjoying life with the Italian club, Torino, who had bought him from Manchester City a year earlier.

Busby acted immediately on hearing a whisper that his quicksilver countryman might be available, but the transfer to

a 16-year-old in Scotland's youth team. I was overjoyed to be working for someone I trusted and respected, and it was important that I had been bought to play attacking football, the sort I loved."

As for the manager, although he was a master at masking his true emotions, he could scarcely conceal his glee when

"Denis was the most expensive signing I ever made. But in terms of achievement, he turned out to be the cheapest"

United seemed to have stalled when Law was placed under extreme pressure to join Juventus.

Denis takes up the story: "It was even threatened that I would never play again if I didn't join Juve, which I didn't want to do. I had been anxious because Torino had messed United around and I was afraid that Matt Busby might not come back.

"When the deal went through, for what was then a British record of £115,000, I felt overwhelming relief. I knew Matt pretty well, having seen him on and off since I was

reminiscing in later years: "Denis was the most expensive signing I ever made. But in terms of sheer achievement, he turned out to be the cheapest. He was the most thrilling player in the game, the quickest thinker on the pitch I ever saw, and the greatest man in the penalty box. Nobody else scored so many miracle goals."

Bobby Charlton was already an Old Trafford hero, and Irish teenager George Best – described on arrival in Manchester as 'a bag of bones with a golden gift' – had overcome a bout of homesickness to

Another piece of the jigsaw as Pat Crerand signs for United in 1963, pictured with Busby, club secretary Les Olive, standing left, and assistant manager Jimmy Murphy

enlist. Thus Busby was well on the way to assembling what would enter football folklore as 'The United Trinity', still by some distance, after all these years, unquestionably the most breathtakingly gifted British threesome ever to come together under the banner of a single club.

But as 1962/63 unfolded, it became clear that there would be trauma on the way to renaissance. That term Busby, while searching for a winning blend, presided over a tense relegation battle during which he was not helped by uneasy relationships between some of his players.

Wilf McGuinness, then a coach at the club and eventually Matt's ill-starred successor as manager, recalls that testing time: "At one point there were even mutterings in the press about Matt being sacked. To me, and to the players, this was unthinkable, and we viewed the mere suggestion as an outrage."

"At one point there were even mutterings in the press about Matt being sacked. We viewed the mere suggestion as an outrage"

David Herd, third right, scores United's second goal in the '63 FA Cup final triumph; (below) Johnny Giles

The man himself remained a monument to dignity, exuding moral strength as he went quietly but charismatically about his business, and duly guided United clear of the drop, albeit with only three points to spare.

If the acquisition of Law was one masterstroke, then another was paying Celtic £53,000 for the mid-season transfer of Paddy Crerand, the sublimely creative but occasionally volcanic Scottish international wing-half who became one of the most influential members of the team for the rest of Busby's career.

The newly-signed pair were both key performers as United finished a disappointing term on a glorious high by winning the FA Cup. On a golden afternoon in late May – the season was running late following one of the harshest winters on record – United beat strong favourites Leicester City 3-1 with one goal from Law and two from David Herd, their moves flitting like sunshine across Wembley's velvet green carpet.

Busby beamed benevolently as his Red Devils entertained royally and collected their first trophy since Munich. His revolution was progressing, but there were still stormy days ahead before his latest dazzling creation was complete.

One pressing problem concerned John Giles, an immensely skilful, acutely intelligent and stoutly forthright young footballer who would eventually mature into one of the supreme midfield playmakers of his era. The trouble was that, at least partly due to hot competition for places, Busby often played Giles on the wing, where the Dubliner was far from happy. Beyond that, there was a personality clash. The two men simply did not get on. As Giles later wrote: "As far as Matt was concerned, everything I did was wrong."

The situation was resolved with the 22-year-old's £33,000 transfer to Leeds United in August 1963, and later Busby would admit, with characteristic grace, that the sale of Giles was the biggest mistake of his career.

The popular notion of 'The Old Man', as the manager was widely known, as warmly benign was not misleading in essence, but it concealed his underlying steel, as noted vividly by one of his most loyal retainers, centre-half Bill Foulkes.

"Matt Busby didn't wield his

United players celebrate after young George Best, far left, scores his first league goal for the Reds in a Division One match against Burnley at Old Trafford in December 1963

all-encompassing power through being a soft touch. Underneath that avuncular demeanour was a seriously ruthless character. This may surprise many people, given the public image of the two men, but the main difference between Matt and Alex Ferguson, was that Alex, for all his famous drive and aggression, leavened his approach with a touch of forgiveness. Matt had none whatsoever. He would not be swayed by anyone, and all disagreements had to end in his favour or the other party, sooner or later, would be leaving the club."

For all that, Big Bill held his mentor in deep affection and respect: "He could be overwhelmingly kind, he appeared to have the wisdom of Solomon, he was perhaps the cleverest man I ever met, and I have never known anyone with such imposing personal presence. He had an enormous influence on my career, seeing something in me which perhaps others might have missed, and I owe him more than words can express."

Unexpectedly in view of the FA Cup triumph, United started the 1963/64 season in abject fashion, being thrashed 4-0 by champions Everton in the Charity Shield. Busby reacted boldly, axing Giles, inside-right Albert Quixall and centre-forward David Herd from the team and giving youth its chance in the form of three rookie forwards, Ian Moir, Phil Chisnall and David Sadler. The trio did well before being withdrawn in the autumn to develop further in the Reserves, but it was the impact of an even younger newcomer, George Best, that was most dramatic.

Busby knew the boy from Belfast was special, even by Old Trafford standards, and after a promising debut at home to West Bromwich Albion in September, George was pitched into a return match with Burnley in late December, two days after the Reds had been hammered 6-1 at Turf Moor. Best scintillated as United took their revenge to the tune of 5-1, and he remained a fixture in the team for the remainder of that season (and far beyond).

Now Busby, crucially aided as ever by Jimmy Murphy, was at the helm of a rapidly improving combination that finished the '63/64 campaign as runners-up to Bill Shankly's Liverpool in the title race.

Admittedly they were smarting from two numbing knockout setbacks, a 3-1 FA Cup semi-final defeat to West Ham on

a Hillsborough quagmire followed four days later by a stunning 5-0 evisceration by Sporting Lisbon in the last four of the European Cup Winners' Cup – and that after leading 4-1 from the first leg.

However, the ever-sagacious Busby saw beyond the setbacks, recognised that he was on the right track, and acquired two new faces for the 1964/65 campaign, which was to end with the league championship pennant fluttering over Old Trafford for the first time since the air crash.

One was goalkeeper Pat Dunne, who cost £10,000 from Shamrock Rovers, received an unexpectedly prompt first-team opportunity through injuries to Harry Gregg and David Gaskell, then made the most of his fortune by retaining his place until the title medals were handed out. The other was England international winger John Connelly, a superbly penetrative raider and workaholic tackler-back who had already collected a title gong with Burnley in 1959/60 and would contribute 20 goals during the season, 15 of them

in league combat. Connelly, another straight-talker in the Giles mould who would eventually leave after differences with Busby, was also a supremely dedicated professional whose impeccable attitude would prove invaluable.

It was a term in which the manager wrought another crucial change, the switching of Bobby Charlton from the left wing, where he had not been content, to a deep-lying central role in which he linked exquisitely with Crerand, the pair passing the ball beautifully and Charlton continuing to contribute explosive striking power, often from spectacularly long range.

Busby paid the unassuming North-Easterner the ultimate compliment when he declared that in midfield "his game is now very reminiscent of Alfredo di Stefano's". As for Bobby, he was relieved: "I used to loathe having to stand near the touchline waiting for the ball, which wasn't my natural game. I loved running and always had loads of energy, so I wanted to be in the thick of the action.

Clockwise from left: skipper Denis Law shakes hands with Leeds captain Bobby Collins before the 1965 FA Cup semi-final match at Hillsborough; United in action against Ferencvaros in the first leg of the Inter-Cities Fairs Cup semi-final; Law is carried aloft as he holds the Football League trophy after 1964/65 triumph; the joyous scenes that led to that title, as Law scores his club's third goal against Arsenal in late April

Busby displayed his managerial nous with decisive results. Denis Law had ripped his knee while starring in a 3-0 victory at Anfield 48 hours earlier, yet there were press reports predicting that he would have to be restrained physically from facing the Gunners on the night that could virtually confirm United as champions.

Denis recalls: "Excuse me! I had just had six stitches in the joint, which was extremely tender, and I thought there was absolutely no way I should be playing. But Matt Busby would have none of it. When I gaped and pointed at my knee, he just said: 'Ah, you'll be all right. Just get out there and play.' So what choice did I have?"

Duly the wound was sprayed to deaden the pain, Law scored twice in a 3-1 triumph and the manager was vindicated. Denis again: "Afterwards Matt just smiled and said: 'Well done, son. I knew you'd be all right!'"

That term United also reached two semi-finals, bowing out of the FA Cup to Leeds after two ferocious battles which saw both teams criticised for their

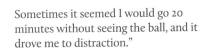

Sometimes it seemed I would go 20 minutes without seeing the ball, and it drove me to distraction."

In central defence, meanwhile, Foulkes and Stiles became a reassuringly effective settled pair, with Bill snuffing out the majority of aerial threats while Nobby, vastly underrated as an all-round footballer

"I loved running and always had loads of energy, so I wanted to be in the thick of the action"

because of his famous abrasive qualities, read the unfolding action superbly.

United vied with Leeds and Chelsea for most of the season, finally claiming the crown – barring the miracle of a 19-goal defeat by Aston Villa in their last match – in the penultimate game, in which Arsenal were defeated 3-1 at Old Trafford. It was an occasion on which

untrammelled physicality, and exiting the Inter-Cities Fairs Cup – the modern equivalent is the Europa League – at the hands of Ferencvaros, but only after a play-off in Hungary.

Following all that, it was widely anticipated that 1965/66 would be a vintage season for Busby's team, which appeared to be peaking irresistibly. There were no

George Best's star turn in the 5-1 hammering of Benfica in Lisbon; (right) Busby in good spirits following United's 1967 title triumph

new major transfer investments, but with youngsters such as utility man David Sadler, who was destined to become an England centre-half but had not yet settled to his optimum position, and wingers John Aston junior and Jim Ryan progressing encouragingly, the manager was satisfied with his squad. In addition, Harry Gregg had fought back from horrendous injury problems to reclaim his place between the sticks, and the prospects of further success appeared to be rosy.

United went flat-out for what would have been an astonishing Treble, only to falter agonisingly in the late stages of all three competitions. The league title was annexed by Liverpool, with Manchester's Reds slipping back to fourth. Busby's men reached the last four of the FA Cup for the fifth year in succession, only to lose 1-0 to Everton at Burnden Park, and they fell 2-1 on aggregate to Partizan Belgrade in the semi-final of the European Cup.

The defeat by the combative but essentially unremarkable Yugoslavians was the most galling of all, given that it followed what was surely United's most majestic ever performance on foreign soil. In the quarter-finals they had been paired with Benfica,

Lisbon's mighty Eagles, who had contested four of the previous five European Cup finals, lifting the trophy twice.

After United had won the first leg at Old Trafford by a slender 3-2 margin, common wisdom had it that they were doomed to defeat. But Busby knew they were still in with a decent chance and during his pre-match instructions at the Stadium of Light, he cautioned his players to "keep it tight" for the first 20 minutes, then see what developed.

Evidently Best had not been listening.

"United went flat out for what would have been an astonishing Treble"

After 15 minutes, Matt's men were 3-0 up, with the ungovernable Irishman having netted first with a perfectly judged looping header, then with a low shot after waltzing past several defenders 'like a dark ghost', as the revered *Times* writer Geoffrey Green described it. Next, for good measure, Best set up the third goal for John Connelly and United ran out 5-1 winners on the night, 8-3 on aggregate, having humbled one of

the finest sides in European football history in front of 75,000 fans.

Afterwards Matt Busby, modest as ever but justifiably proud, declared: "This was our finest hour." Best recalled: "I felt superb. The atmosphere sent the blood coursing through my veins. It seemed to add power to my muscles, imagination to my brain. Every time I looked up there seemed to be nobody but a United man to pass to. I couldn't go wrong."

Now the Reds were scorching hot favourites for the glittering prize, but what awaited them was dismal anti-climax. Though Best was struggling with a knee problem that would ultimately demand an operation, Busby opted to gamble on his talismanic sprite for the first game in Belgrade. It backfired, the Irishman battling valiantly but unable to make his customary

impact. Law, Foulkes and Stiles were also carrying injuries so the team was well below par, losing 2-0 in Yugoslavia and managing only a 1-0 win at home.

Foulkes later lamented: "Although we had a very fine team, a great one even, we never had sufficient depth of squad as we had before the crash. That meant that almost every season, come the spring, perhaps half of us were playing when almost crippled with niggling injuries. As a result, we experienced collective burn-out. How we would have relished the rest that another couple of high-quality team-mates would have afforded. We won plenty, but we could have achieved so much more with a bigger pool of players."

Despite such debilitating disappointment, Busby and Murphy picked up their team's spirits to such

Clockwise from left: toasting the 1966/67 title in the Upton Park dressing room; parading the trophy a week later at Old Trafford; goalmouth action against Partizan Belgrade in the previous campaign's European Cup semi-final; Law scoring in the victorious quarter-final

uplifting effect that they regained the league championship in 1966/67, but not before the Old Man had dealt skilfully with a potentially thorny situation when Denis Law asked for a transfer during the preceding summer.

With a mischievous grin, Denis casts his mind back: "All I wanted was an extra tenner a week! If a Premier League footballer of today found one of those in his pocket, probably he'd use it to light his cigar. When I apologised publicly for asking for a rise, it seemed like I was backing down, but in private I was given my tenner. Saying sorry was merely an exercise in saving Matt's face. In the end we were both happy – I didn't want to go and he didn't want to sell me."

With that settled, Busby made the shrewd signing of goalkeeper Alex Stepney from Chelsea, the Londoner hitting such superlative form almost immediately that his delighted manager reckoned he was the decisive factor in the title triumph.

On the debit side that term, there was the loss of Connelly to Blackburn Rovers following a clash of opinions with the manager, though that was mitigated by the continued rise of Aston junior, while the adaptable Sadler also shone in several positions.

Sadly, there was heartbreak, too, with young left-back Bobby Noble, a tough-as-nails local boy who had been tipped for a long-term international future, being invalided out of the game due to horrific injuries sustained in a car crash in April.

Only two weeks after the luckless 21-year-old began a long and courageous but ultimately unsuccessful bid to recover full fitness, United clinched the league crown with a sumptuous 6-1 victory at West Ham and Busby's thoughts turned again to his ultimate goal. After the Partizan defeat, and with his lovely team beginning to age, he feared that he might never have another

chance of fulfilling his dream.

With his whole being, Matt wanted the European Cup, partly as any manager would covet the top prize in the club game. But on a more personal level it was as if winning the trophy would be making some sense of the ground-breaking journey on which he had set out in 1956, and which had, albeit through no fault of his own, cost the lives of so many fine young men whom he had loved like sons.

There was also the little matter of

of Europe proved even more dramatic. With the dashing young Mancunian marksman Brian Kidd a prominent addition to the attacking mix, United began the Continental campaign in almost gentle style, disposing of Hibernians of Malta 4-0 on aggregate in the first round.

The next steps on their march to glory were rather more demanding. It took two grindingly attritional battles to beat FC Sarajevo of Yugoslavia 2-1 in the

"That was a marvellous piece of psychology by Matt. It lifted our heads, gave us a fresh perspective, then Real played into our hands by showboating"

successfully defending the league title in 1967/68, and for much of the season United looked set to accomplish that, topping the table from November to March, then returning to the pinnacle in April, only to slip up at the death, with the crown crossing Manchester to Maine Road only on the final day.

Their fourth bid to become champions

second round, then the Polish champions, Gornik Zabrze, provided tough and polished quarter-final opposition. The Reds prevailed 2-0 at Old Trafford, courtesy of an own goal and a cute Kidd back-heel in the dying minutes, then mounted a stirring rearguard action on a treacherous surface in front of 105,000 fans in snowbound Silesia, losing by the

contest's only goal but again progressing 2-1 over two legs.

Now, despite the failure of fitness gambles two years earlier, Busby took another massive chance by naming his skipper, Law, to face Real Madrid in the home leg of the semi-final, though the plucky Scot was severely handicapped by knee trouble. Best supplied the game's only goal with a bullet drive from a clever Aston pull-back, but that seemed a perilously slender lead to take to Spain.

It appeared that once again the Bernabéu would be the graveyard of Busby's aspirations as Real led 3-1 at half-time. But the United boss used the interval to revive sagging spirits, reminding his men that they were only one down over the two games. As Bill Foulkes put it: "That was a marvellous piece of psychology by Matt. It lifted our heads, gave us a fresh perspective, then Real played into our hands by showboating."

Duly United clung on, then Sadler stunned Madrid by nudging home a scrappy overall equaliser some 20 minutes from the end. Now the Spaniards were psychologically on the floor and the Reds capitalised in startling fashion, Best dancing down the right touchline before crossing for Foulkes, of all people, to slot home unerringly.

Bill recalled: "I didn't score many goals, and this seemed unreal, as if I was frozen in time. When my team-mates mobbed me, my reaction was to tell Nobby to stay back because there were still 15 minutes to go – he called me a miserable bugger!"

The veteran stopper, the team's longest server, needn't have worried. The tie finished 4-3 in United's favour and there were uncharacteristic tears of joy, relief and goodness knows what other complicated emotions in the dressing room from Busby, who for some moments could only mutter: "I can't help it! I can't help it!" Later the Old Man asked Foulkes – with whom he shared a special bond, the pair having survived Munich together – what on earth he'd been doing in Real's box, and the centre-half could give no rational explanation, offering only: "It was 10 years on from Munich. It must have been destiny."

George Best, resplendent in United blue, in action in the final against Benfica at a packed Wembley

And so to a balmy May evening at Wembley, where the blue-shirted Reds stepped out to face old foes Benfica in the final of the European Cup. With Law sidelined by a knee operation – poor Denis was practically demented at missing the biggest match in the club's history – Charlton took on the captaincy, an appropriate honour for another crash survivor.

The first half was a tense affair, with Best and Portuguese star Eusebio both being singled out for bone-crunching tackles that might have intimidated lesser men but which merely sharpened the determination of this sparkling pair to carry their respective sides to victory.

Eusebio went closest to a goal before the interval when he set Stepney's crossbar shivering from long range, while the otherwise splendid Sadler stabbed United's best chance wide of a post.

The deadlock was broken early in the second period when Charlton met a tantalising Sadler cross with a perfect glancing header. As the match wore on, with young Aston terrorising the Benfica rearguard with his searing pace, Busby's men seemed the more likely victors, only for Jaime Graca to equalise 10 minutes from the end. Now United might have crumbled, and three minutes from time it appeared they had done just that as Eusebio, for once giving his ferocious jailer Stiles the slip, bore down on goal with only Stepney to beat. A Benfica winner seemed inevitable, but instead of placing the ball safely into the net, the Portuguese went for the spectacular option, hammering a shot which thudded into the keeper's midriff, where he clutched it gratefully.

That crisis negotiated, Busby came into his own during the brief interlude ahead of extra time. Exuding calmness, he urged his tired players to observe the sagging body language of their opponents. "They are beaten," he told them. "Now just go and finish the job."

But even Matt could hardly have envisaged how rapidly his few eloquent words would galvanise his team. Within 10 minutes United had swept aside all semblance of Benfica resistance, Best commencing the unstoppable surge in a manner befitting his genius. Stepney launched a long clearance, Kidd nodded it on and the Irishman swerved beyond a posse of back-pedalling defenders, feinted past keeper Jose Henrique and tucked the ball between the unattended posts.

Some 60 seconds later, Kidd celebrated his 19th birthday by netting with a header at the second attempt, then soon sent in Charlton to complete the 4-1 rout with an adroit finish. After that, in the words of Bobby, "everything else was like a visit to paradise".

When the final whistle blew, Busby was engulfed, understandably enough but so overwhelmingly that Charlton was initially concerned: "I almost felt the need to check he was all right, but seeing his wide grin I held back until the hectic activity had calmed down a bit. Eventually I reached him and gave him a long hug. There was absolutely no need for words. It had been his pioneering team that had

been devastated on the European trail, and this was their symbolic rebirth. Tears were shed and nothing could bring back the lives that had been lost, but here, at least, was some sort of balance, perhaps even a degree of closure."

After the final whistle, Busby himself reflected on the events of extra time with frank amazement: "We had won but it seemed to have come so suddenly after the years of waiting. Half an hour ago we were on the knife-edge. What a difference 30 little minutes can make! I had a brief thought about Benfica, so near and yet so far. It lasted about three seconds and then emotion set in."

As the drinks flowed freely at the celebration banquet, most of which was missed by Charlton and Crerand because their strenuous midfield exertions on such a stiflingly hot evening had left them severely dehydrated, Matt treated the revellers to a heartfelt rendition of Louis Armstrong's *What A Wonderful World.* And that night, for everybody who held Manchester United close to their hearts, that said it all.

Busby with his beloved trophy the day after final triumph, about to take it back from London to Manchester to celebrate; (left) extra-time inspiration from the manager

Busby's three greatest teams

Busby is considered to have created three great teams during the course of his time as United manager – his first trophy winners, his beloved 'Babes' of the mid-to-late 1950s and his title and European Cup-winning side a decade on. Here's an overview of each of those three sides, the key members and what they achieved...

FIRST GREAT TEAM 1948 FA CUP AND 1952 TITLE WINNERS

Charlie Mitten   Stan Pearson   Jack Rowley   Johnny Morris   Jimmy Delaney

Henry Cockburn   Allenby Chilton   John Anderson

John Aston Snr   Johnny Carey

Jack Crompton

Also:
Reg Allen,
Billy McGlen,
John Downie

When Busby became United manager, he inherited a squad of talented players, many of whom had come through the MUJAC youth team. His skill with his first great side was in recognising that talent, in drawing the best from it, and in adding a little bit on top. Of the above XI, which started the 1948 FA Cup final, only Jimmy Delaney was a Busby addition, signed from Celtic in February 1946. The core of this team went on to win the league title in 1951/1952, with the help of a few extra signings such as John Downie and Reg Allen, and an injection of youth in the shape of Johnny Berry and Roger Byrne, who broke through that season.

SECOND GREAT TEAM 1956 AND 1957 TITLE WINNERS

David Pegg

Dennis Viollet

Tommy Taylor

Billy Whelan

Johnny Berry

Duncan Edwards

Jackie Blanchflower

Eddie Colman

Roger Byrne

Bill Foulkes

Also:
Mark Jones,
Wilf McGuinness,
Albert Scanlon

Ray Wood

Busby had allowed his first great team to grow old gracefully – and successfully – knowing that he had an unbelievable bounty of young players emerging beneath them. His famous 'Busby Babes' took the nation by storm, playing bold and freewheeling football that accrued consecutive titles in 1955/56 and 1956/57 (almost a Double that year too, denied in the FA Cup final by Aston Villa and Peter McParlane's notorious shoulder-charge on Ray Wood). This second great Busby side was halted in its young, trailblazing tracks by the Munich disaster.

THIRD GREAT TEAM 1965 AND 1967 TITLE WINNERS, 1968 EUROPEAN CUP WINNERS

John Aston Jr

David Herd

George Best

Denis Law

Bobby Charlton

Nobby Stiles

Bill Foulkes

Pat Crerand

Tony Dunne

Shay Brennan

Also:
John Connelly,
Harry Gregg,
Brian Kidd,
David Sadler,
Maurice Setters

Alex Stepney

Arguably Busby's greatest achievement was in rebuilding after Munich to create a third all-conquering side. It took time but Busby slowly assembled the pieces – Charlton was already in situ, Law was added for a record fee, Best exploded from the youth ranks, Crerand arrived from Celtic. After an early iteration of this team won the 1963 FA Cup, it developed further to win league titles in 1964/65 and 1966/7 and finally, emotionally, to reach the zenith of Busby's rein by capturing the hallowed European Cup in 1968.

Chapter 7

The long goodbye

Having transformed United into the Continental conquerors he had long envisaged, Busby's brilliant building blocks tumbled into an era of decline. Long after his second retirement, though, the club's rightful place among Europe's elite would be re-established by another visionary Scot

Busby was knighted following the European Cup victory in 1968, before being made a Knight Commander of St Gregory by the Pope in 1972

Welcoming new manager
Frank O'Farrell to Old
Trafford in July 1971;
(below) Busby had
announced his
retirement in 1969

The sense of closure afforded by victory at Wembley was inevitable after the harrowing path taken by Busby's United in reaching the peak of European football. Few could have foreseen, however, the speed of the Reds' descent after experiencing such highs.

The manager was knighted in the wake of United's European Cup success, adding the honour to his existing OBE and his status as a Freeman of Manchester, but he had gained a new ambition in football. "There remained only one competition to win," he said, as his European champions prepared to enter the World Club Championship, a two-legged meeting with South American counterparts Estudiantes. Though currently recognised by FIFA as the height of world club football, the showpiece was far from a prestigious affair back in September 1968, having previously been marred by violent clashes between rival players. United's participation hardly drew unanimous acclaim, yet Busby stressed: "Football is a world game and I do not think that a problem can be solved by running away from it."

The tone for a seething fixture was set during the first leg in Argentina, where

Denis Law, who appeared to have levelled the aggregate score against AC Milan in the European Cup semi-final. The Scot's effort was ruled not to have crossed the line, however, ending United's reign as kings of Europe with a 1-2 defeat. Allied to an 11th-place First Division finish and an immediate future without Continental football, the landscape ahead looked flat. No more Everests to conquer.

The future would also be bereft of Busby, in a managerial capacity at least. He had announced in January 1969 that he would be standing down as boss, 23 years after first arriving at Old Trafford. "I had had enough," he ventured. "Manchester United had become a world-famous organisation,

> "Manchester United had become a world-famous organisation, and the demands had grown every year"

headbutts, punches and kicks were thrown by the hosts, before Nobby Stiles was red-carded for contesting a linesman's offside decision. Back at Old Trafford, Estudiantes increased their 1-0 aggregate lead through Juan Ramon Veron (father of future Reds midfielder Juan Sebastian), and Best and Hugo Medina were dismissed for fighting. Willie Morgan's goal proved to be nothing more than a consolation, as Brian Kidd's apparently legitimate late strike was disallowed in controversial circumstances.

Later in the season, a similar fate befell

and the demands had grown every year from the start until it had reached far beyond the power, the energy or the capacity of one man to do."

The agreed solution was for the Scot to continue in a new role as general manager, with a younger successor taking over team affairs. "The board agreed with my recommendation to give a chance to Wilf McGuinness who, young as he was, had made his way as a coach and had been with the club straight from school. As it turned out, it was a mistake," Matt later conceded.

Sir Matt and Bobby Charlton take on some schoolchildren in 1970

The theories behind United's slump under McGuinness varied. "It was a psychological blow to everybody that Matt wasn't the manager any more," said veteran midfielder Paddy Crerand. Busby saw an unhealthy dynamic between the new manager and his former team-mates, saying: "Wilf's mistakes were in his handling of players he had been brought up with. It is my opinion, too, that he was then too inexperienced to handle them and get full response."

Despite reaching three cup semi-finals in a season-and-a-half in charge, McGuinness' tenure came to an end in December 1970, with United fifth from bottom of Division One. Busby was accused by the media of meddling in his successor's stewardship, especially after his reluctant agreement to return to the manager's position until the end of the 1970/71 season. "I can assure my doubters that I did not want to take the team reins again," he stressed.

The Scot's return began with an FA Cup defeat to Middlesbrough, but a swift upturn in league fortunes culminated in an eighth-place finish, rounded off by a 4-3 win over Manchester City at Maine Road in which Denis Law, Bobby Charlton and George Best (2) fittingly all struck. Charlton reflected: "I had the satisfaction of feeling that, on his last day as the

"On his last day as manager, Matt had been reminded of what his work would always represent"

manager of Manchester United, Matt had almost certainly been reminded of what his work would always represent most strikingly: a willingness to nourish talented players, to give them freedom to express all their ability."

Having led player discussions, captain Charlton later approached Busby to

Charlton's service to
United is honoured as
he plays his final league
game for the club in April
1973; (below) Busby
marvels at the Premier
League trophy in the
Old Trafford dressing
room in May 1993

implore him to continue in the role,
only for the Scot to respond: "Bobby,
this is one of the nicest things that ever
happened to me and I am very grateful,
but I've had enough."

Busby duly handed over to Frank
O'Farrell and took a place on the board of
directors. He remained in the role until
1982, thereafter becoming club president,
and watched from an elevated position
as the club toiled to rediscover the glories
it had experienced during his quarter-
century in charge.

Sporadic success punctuated a
comparatively fallow period through
the tenures of Tommy Docherty, Dave
Sexton and Ron Atkinson, before the 1986
appointment of Alex Ferguson. "Sir Matt
was extremely supportive when I arrived
at Old Trafford," said Ferguson. "I was in
awe of the man because for such a famous
figure he was so humble and unassuming,
a wonderfully warm man. He didn't offer
any suggestions regarding the running
of the team but the welcome he gave me
was marvellous and he helped me to settle
down at the club. 'If you ever need me, you
know where I am,' he said to me soon after
I arrived at Old Trafford. I never forgot it
and I never will."

Silverware took three full seasons to
rematerialise at Old Trafford, and 1990's
FA Cup success proved to be the first drips
of a torrent of success. For Busby, the
greatest joy was witnessing the end of a
26-year wait to emulate his 1966/67 First
Division triumph, as the Reds won the
inaugural Premier League title in 1992/93.

"I remember he joined us in the dressing
room after the last home game against
Blackburn Rovers and all the lads had
their photograph taken with him and the
Premier League trophy," recalled Ferguson.
He enjoyed the occasion as much as they
did – nothing was too much trouble. There
was a shine in his eyes that night; he was so
happy. He had seen his beloved United win
the title again."

Chapter 8

An enduring legacy

Sir Matt's passing was followed by an incredibly poignant afternoon at Old Trafford as everyone connected with Manchester United paid their respects. While more than 20 years have now passed since he left us, his achievements ensure he will never be forgotten

On 20 January, 1994, just 264 days after seeing his club retake the throne of English football, Sir Matt Busby passed away in his sleep, losing a long battle against cancer and setting in motion one of the most poignant mass outpourings of grief Manchester has known.

In the same manner that a silent Old Trafford vigil followed the Munich Air Disaster, scores of emotional United fans traversed Sir Matt Busby Way – née Warwick Road – to pay tribute to the most important figure in the club's history.

By the time of the Reds' next game, a Premier League meeting with Everton two days later, the stadium forecourt was awash with tributes, as colours of other clubs bobbed in a sea of red and white scarves, shirts, flags and flowers. "A day when the overwhelming echoes of history came blowing on the wind across Old Trafford," reflected *The Daily Telegraph*, of an afternoon of raw emotion which swelled and wrenched hearts in equal measure.

"It was one of those days that will live on in the memory forever," admitted Rodger Gifford, referee on the most sombre of occasions. "I was getting ready for the game

and Alex Ferguson, whose room was near ours, came in, sat down next to me and asked: 'What sort of game are you hoping for today?' I said: 'One which would make Sir Matt Busby proud,' and he just nodded.

"Standing at the top of the tunnel before we went out, the silence was absolutely surreal. Normally if you're at any game, whether it's parks football or the Premier League, there's a buzz in the air. But to

"Matt always had a smile on his face even during the last few days in hospital. For champions past and present, please sing the roof off the stadium today"

stand there in the tunnel 10 minutes before kick-off, look out and not hear a sound was just incredible."

Pin-drop silence soundtracked stadium announcer Keith Fane's reading of a pre-match message from the Busby family. "Matt always had a smile on his face even during the last few days in hospital," it said. "For champions past and present, please sing the roof off the stadium today." The roar

United and Everton players stand with their heads bowed during the minute's silence in honour of Sir Matt Busby. Right, from top: a lone piper leads the teams out; the funeral cortege pauses outside Old Trafford; a shrine of tributes outside the stadium

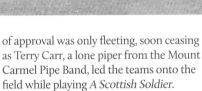

of approval was only fleeting, soon ceasing as Terry Carr, a lone piper from the Mount Carmel Pipe Band, led the teams onto the field while playing *A Scottish Soldier*.

The match, an undercard event beneath the tribute to a departed figurehead, became an exhibition display from a United side briskly defending their title and already 16 points clear at the head of the Premier League table. "Everybody who was on that pitch wanted to pay their own tribute to one of the greatest managers of all time," said Gifford, who oversaw a game in which the Reds thrilled throughout and Ryan Giggs scored the only goal. "My philosophy as a referee was quite simply if they wanted to play, let them get on with it. By God, did they get on with it! It was at such a pace. It flowed, nobody argued, they got on with it and it was a superb advert for the game; one of the finest games of football I've ever participated in. At the final whistle, walking off, Sir Alex appeared beside me, shook my hand and just said: 'You got your wish, son. We paid the old man a good tribute today.'"

More would follow. Asked after his retirement if it would be permissible to have his work commemorated by a statue at Old Trafford, Busby declined

Fans hold up a tribute to Sir Matt Busby ahead of the 2009 Champions League final; (below) his bronze memorial looks out from the East Stand

and insisted: "My memorial is the three great teams I created." Nevertheless, his bronze likeness was unveiled in 1996 and positioned beneath the glass frontage of the East Stand – or Scoreboard End, as he would have known it – presiding over all visitors to the club. In 2008, he was joined on the forecourt by his United Trinity, with Best, Law and Charlton also immortalised and fittingly placed under their manager's watchful gaze.

Tributes have ranged from off-field gestures to on-field feats. In 1999, on what would have been his 90th birthday, the near-miraculous heroics of Ferguson's side in securing an unprecedented Treble in Barcelona were quickly earmarked as a fitting homage. "I think he was up there doing a lot of kicking," joked Ferguson, whose side were met by an enormous mosaic of Busby's face a decade later when they took to the field for the 2009 Champions League final in Rome.

Sir Matt is never far from the mind at United. His vision of a club renowned

Sir Matt joins fellow knight Sir Alex Ferguson as they parade their European silverware in 1991; (left) Robin van Persie collects the club's Sir Matt Busby Player of the Year trophy in 2013

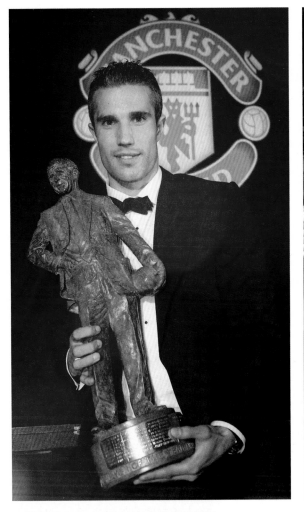

around the world has long since been realised, owing greatly to his groundwork. The bomb-shattered Old Trafford he visited upon taking charge has been rebuilt as the grandest setting in British club football. A pioneer on the business side of the club as well as the football side, he introduced corporate hospitality viewing to English football, while the work he

talents playing for the love of the game and freedom of expression have been passed from generation to generation, with supporters young and old clear in their demands for 'football taught by Matt Busby,' when singing the *United Calypso*. The Babes, Munich and Wembley may have happened a lifetime ago, even before the majority of modern supporters were born,

"I'm privileged to have followed Sir Matt because all you have to do is to try and maintain the standards that he set"

did with his players set in stasis the club's standards of success, playing ethos and youth development. As Sir Alex succinctly put it: "I'm privileged to have followed Sir Matt because all you have to do is to try and maintain the standards that he set so many years ago."

But it is in the stands that Busby's legacy is most animated. The tales of gifted

but it is easy to cling tightly to a heritage so steeped in goodness and inspiration.

From humble roots to glory, via graft, drama and tragedy. The stories of Manchester United and Sir Matt Busby are mirrored and entwined in perpetuity, and as long as this club exists, so too will the legend of the man who did more for it than any other.

VITAL STATISTICS

Busby's glorious reign was about so much more than figures, tallies and tables, but these numbers make for fascinating reading...

COMPLETE MANAGERIAL RECORD

PLAYED: 1,141
WON: 576
DREW: 266
LOST: 299
SCORED: 2,324
CONCEDED: 1,566
WIN RATIO: 50.48%
DRAW RATIO: 23.31%
LOSS RATIO: 26.21%

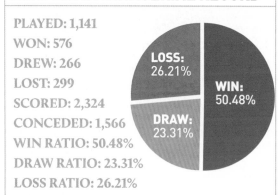

LOSS: 26.21%
WIN: 50.48%
DRAW: 23.31%

MANAGERIAL HONOURS

EUROPEAN CUP: 1967/68
FIRST DIVISION: 1951/52, 1955/56, 1956/57, 1964/65, 1966/67
FA CUP: 1948, 1963
CHARITY SHIELD: 1952, 1956, 1957, 1965 (shared), 1967 (shared)

LANDMARK GAMES

FIRST
05/01/1946 – ACCRINGTON S. 2 UNITED 2

500
18/02/1957 – CHARLTON 1 UNITED 5

100
01/09/1948 – UNITED 3 BLACKPOOL 4

1,000
12/11/1966 – UNITED 2 SHEFF WED 0

250
22/09/1951 – TOTTENHAM 2 UNITED 0

LAST
05/05/1971 – CITY 3 UNITED 4

OLD TRAFFORD RECORD

*Maine Road was United's home ground for Busby's first three seasons at the club

P	491
W	317
D	96
L	78
GF	1,148
GA	528

GOALS GALORE:

 **77** players scored for United under Busby, whose side also benefited from **38** own goals during his tenure

TOP 5 GOALSCORERS:

| Law – 211 | Charlton – 210 | Rowley – 190 | Viollet – 179 | Herd – 145 |

TOP GOALSCORER MOST SEASONS UNDER BUSBY:

Rowley & Law
(Five seasons each)

Number of players used under Busby **129**

TOP 5 APPEARANCE-MAKERS UNDER BUSBY

| Foulkes – 685 | Charlton – 578 | T Dunne – 398 | Chilton – 391 | Stiles – 368 |

RECORD TRANSFER FEE PAID

£110,000

for Denis Law from Torino (1962) and Willie Morgan from Burnley (1968)

143

Most goals in a single season in all competitions: 1956/57

TOTAL ATTENDANCE FOR UNITED GAMES UNDER BUSBY

49,978,922 SUPPORTERS

HOMEGROWN HEROES

The theme of promoting youth underscored Busby's entire reign at Old Trafford. John Roach made his bow in the Scot's first game in charge, an FA Cup tie with Accrington Stanley, while Tommy O'Neil debuted in Busby's farewell, a 4-3 victory at Manchester City.

HOME COMFORT

United were unbeaten at home in European competition during Busby's time in charge, winning 24 and drawing four of 28 games played at Old Trafford and Maine Road.

MANCHESTER IS *PEOPLE*, MANCHESTER UNITED IS *PEOPLE* AND THE STRETFORD END IS *PEOPLE*, AND SALFORD IS *PEOPLE*. IF THERE ARE WARMER *PEOPLE* THAN THESE, I IN MY TRAVELS MANY TIMES AROUND THE WORLD HAVE NOT MET **THEM.**

— SIR MATT BUSBY —